CREATIVE —PARTY— COOKERY

CREATIVE
PARTY COOKERY

Front cover photograph by Dave Jordan shows
Creamy Chicken Mousse (page 48), Party-time Sandwich Shapes (page 22)
and Melon Cocktails (page 17)

Published 1986 on behalf of
The Boots Company Plc Nottingham England
by Hamlyn Publishing
Bridge House, London Road, Twickenham, Middlesex,
England

ISBN 0 600 32614 4

Set in 10/11pt Gill Sans Light
by Photocomp Ltd, Birmingham

Printed in Italy

Contents

Useful Facts & Figures

Notes on metrication

In this book quantities are given in metric and Imperial measures. Exact conversion from Imperial to metric measures does not usually give very convenient working quantities and so the metric measures have been rounded off into units of 25 grams. The table below shows the recommended equivalents.

Ounces	Approx g to nearest whole figure	Recommended conversion to nearest unit of 25
1	28	25
2	57	50
3	85	75
4	113	100
5	142	150
6	170	175
7	198	200
8	227	225
9	255	250
10	283	275
11	312	300
12	340	350
13	368	375
14	396	400
15	425	425
16 (1 lb)	454	450
17	482	475
18	510	500
19	539	550
20 (1¼ lb)	567	575

Note: When converting quantities over 20 oz first add the appropriate figures in the centre column, then adjust to the nearest unit of 25. As a general guide, 1 kg (1000 g) equals 2·2 lb or about 2 lb 3 oz. This method of conversion gives good results in nearly all cases, although in certain pastry and cake recipes a more accurate conversion is necessary to produce a balanced recipe.

Liquid measures The millilitre has been used in this book and the following table gives a few examples.

Imperial	Approx ml to nearest whole figure	Recommended ml
¼ pint	142	150 ml
½ pint	283	300 ml
¾ pint	425	450 ml
1 pint	567	600 ml
1½ pints	851	900 ml
1¾ pints	992	1000 ml (1 litre)

Spoon measures All spoon measures given in this book are level unless otherwise stated.

Can sizes At present, cans are marked with the exact (usually to the nearest whole number) metric equivalent of the Imperial weight of the contents, so we have followed this practice when giving can sizes.

Oven temperatures

The table below gives recommended equivalents.

	°C	°F	Gas
Very cool	110	225	¼
	120	250	½
Cool	140	275	1
	150	300	2
Moderate	160	325	3
	180	350	4
Moderately hot	190	375	5
	200	400	6
Hot	220	425	7
	230	450	8
Very hot	240	475	9

Note: *When making any of the recipes in this book, only follow one set of measures as they are not interchangeable.*

Introduction

From the planning and preparation stages right through to waving off the last guest, entertaining at home should be a source of pleasure. Whether your party is a simple or elegant gathering of four or six people for dinner or an elaborate buffet spread for twenty or more, the food should be as attractive as possible. The aim of this book is to offer a selection of interesting recipes which are suitable for all sorts of occasions. Ranging from dinner-party starters through to quick and easy toasted sandwiches or snacks, all the finished dishes are appetising and attractive. For example, even the section on sandwiches offers some ideas for garnishes. This introduction offers information and guidance on planning party menus, kitchen equipment, garnishing and presentation. All the tips and notes here can be applied to dishes throughout the book as well as to your own favourite recipes.

Planning Party Menus

One of the most important points to remember when planning a meal is to keep the cooking and preparation within your capabilities as well as within the limitations of your kitchen or living area. For example it is silly to invite ten friends to an elaborate dinner party if you only have six comfortable dining chairs because four unfortunate individuals will find themselves perched uncomfortably on kitchen stools. Avoid cooking an elaborate four-course buffet for twenty if you do not have adequate kitchen facilities and serving dishes; better to present an excellent selection of cheese, pâté and dips with several different types of bread than to risk overworking yourself and presenting second-rate food.

There are some celebrations which demand a traditional dinner party or buffet meal. If the occasion is less formal then the options for entertaining are many and quite varied. For example, brunch offers a popular and relaxed way of entertaining at weekends. Combining breakfast and lunch in a late-morning meal, brunch can be as simple or elaborate as you like and in warm weather it can be served in the garden. If you want to entertain without preparing vast quantities of food, then a light lunch provides a good opportunity. A hearty home-made soup, served with some bread and cheese makes a welcome winter lunch, a light

fish pâté with crisp toast or crackers and a salad are ideal for warmer weather, or barbecued food is perfect for hot summer days in the garden.

Another favourite, old-fashioned opportunity for entertaining is provided by afternoon tea. In winter some hot crumpets, fruit cake and hot crusty bread with jam would be ideal. For summer tea, try dainty sandwiches, fruit tarts, light sponge cakes and iced tea.

For a change, why not invite friends round for waffles or pancakes, or for a sandwich party? Informal gatherings can be great fun – arrange a selection of different sandwich filling ingredients attractively, have ready plenty of different sorts of bread and butter and allow people to make their own sandwiches.

For a drinks party prepare plenty of snacks and food which people can eat standing up, with a glass in one hand. For a buffet meal, plan one or two main dishes, salads and bread or baked potatoes. Prepare a dessert which is easy to serve. Remember that the food must be easy to eat standing up, so avoid any dishes which require a knife and fork approach.

Plan dinner menus carefully, selecting complementary courses which offer a variety of textures and colours. Choose light and substantial dishes carefully so that the meal is well-balanced.

Kitchen Equipment

Tins and Moulds

A wide variety of baking tins and moulds can be purchased for preparing savoury and sweet dishes. The following guidelines may be of some help if you want to buy useful tins or moulds.

Look for small, fluted bun tins which can be used for baking pastry items as well as cakes. Tiny decorated tins are available for making cocktail snacks; boat-shaped tins, shell-shaped tins or horn-shaped tins are also useful. Tall, castle-shaped tins are known as dariole moulds. Individual Yorkshire pudding tins can be used for making a variety of pies or flans.

Large baking tins also come in a variety of unusual shapes and sizes. Look for loaf tins which have drop-down sides or which can be

Some garnishing ideas

extended to offer a variety of sizes and uses. Raised pie moulds (tins) are used to prepare decorative savoury pies and they also come in a variety of sizes, some large enough to bake pies which will serve twenty to thirty people. Ring tins can be used for baking or for setting cold dishes. Fluted tins, heart-shaped tins and a variety of unusual shaped tins can all be used for baking or for setting cold dishes, for example fish moulds.

Small Gadgets
Biscuit Cutters Animal shapes and seasonal shapes as well as hearts and flowers.
Butter Curlers A small serrated blade which is heated in hot water, then drawn across a block of well-chilled butter to make a crinkled strip which rolls into a curl.
Canelle Knife This consists of a small V-shaped cutting edge which is used to remove strips of peel from fruit or to cut grooves or channels down vegetables such as carrots and cucumber. When sliced, the vegetables make an attractive garnishing ingredient.
Cocktail Cutters Tiny square, diamond and crinkled shapes. Use for cutting small savoury biscuits. Very tiny cutters are known as aspic cutters and these are used for cutting out aspic shapes. Used for vegetables such as carrots, cucumber and radishes for garnishing.

Crinkle cutters A corrugated blade used as a cutter for vegetables such as carrots and cucumber. Also used to slice potatoes or to make chips.
Egg Slicer A hollowed frame holds the hard-boiled eggs. Cutting wires are pulled down to cut the egg into slices.
Melon Ballers Available in two or three sizes, these are used to scoop out the flesh from melons. Also useful for cutting potatoes, cheese or butter.
Pastry Cutters Plain or crinkled, these can be used for a variety of tasks, including biscuit making and cutting out chocolate shapes.
Piping Equipment Nozzles range in size from very large vegetable pipes to tiny nozzles for decorating delicate cakes. Buy nylon or fabric piping bags which can be boiled. Alternatively, piping guns come complete with a range of nozzles.

For delicate work and for piping chocolate make cone-shaped piping bags from greaseproof paper. Take a square of greaseproof paper, fold it in half to make a double-thick triangle. Fold this into a cone shape, securing the ends with sticky tape or staples. Cut off the tip as required.

Garnishing Ideas

For savoury dishes use fresh herbs, either sprigs or chopped, sliced tomatoes, cucumber, radishes or other salad ingredients.

For some hot dishes, pipe a swirled border of creamed potato in an ovenproof dish and bake or grill until golden. Ladle casserole-type dishes into the middle or arrange sliced meat, croquettes or chops overlapping in the middle.

Use sliced lemons or oranges as a garnish. To make twists, make a cut into the middle of the slices, then twist them into a curl.

To make croûtons, trim the crusts off bread slices and cut them into neat cubes. Fry until golden in a mixture of oil and butter. Flavour with chopped fresh herbs or add crushed cloves of garlic to the oil if you like. Alternatively, cut the bread into triangles or circles instead of cubes.

Decorate sweet dishes with fresh fruits, toasted nuts or grated chocolate. Make chocolate curls by carving long curled strips out of a block of chocolate. Pipe swirls of whipped cream on to desserts and add quartered slices of orange or lemon.

Dip rose leaves and tiny violets in a little egg white and coat in caster sugar, then leave until dry. Use to decorate cakes and desserts.

Presentation

Make the dining table look as attractive as possible. Co-ordinating crockery and linen look nice. Alternatively serve the food on a variety of pretty plates and dishes. Add flowers and candles or seasonal decorations. Use doilies under cakes and pies, and line bread baskets with napkins. Remember that the food must look appetising.

First Courses

An attractive and appetising first course will ensure that every dinner party is off to a good start. So instead of serving soup or a simple avocado starter, why not try some of the suggestions in this chapter?

Add a spark of interest right at the beginning of the meal and surprise your guests with Saucy Potato Puffs, Seafood Nests or a Scrambled Egg Starter. The knack of serving food which is a bit different lies in taking some ordinary ingredients and transforming them into an unusual dish. It is not always essential to spend a lot of money on exotic ingredients. If you want to serve a light first course, then try Apple Cocktails, or Spicy Grilled Grapefruit, for example.

Remember when planning a lunchtime party, that offering one or two dishes which are intended as starters is often better than presenting one large, heavy main dish.

TARAMASALATA
SERVES 4-6

100 g/4 oz smoked cod's roe, skin removed
4 slices white bread
3 tablespoons lemon juice
200 ml/7 fl oz olive oil
1 small onion, finely grated
1 teaspoon chopped parsley
Crudités
1 red pepper
1 green pepper
1 yellow pepper
4-6 carrots
4-6 celery sticks
½ small cauliflower

Soak the cod's roe in water for 5 minutes to remove some of the salt, then drain. Trim off and discard the crusts from the bread and soak the slices in about 3 tablespoons water for 2 minutes. Remove and squeeze dry.

Place the cod's roe, bread, lemon juice, oil, onion and parsley in a liquidiser and blend until smooth.

Alternatively, mash the roe, bread, onion and parsley by hand with a fork. When smooth, blend in the lemon juice and olive oil slowly, stirring continuously, until well blended. Beat with a whisk until pink and creamy. Chill thoroughly.

Meanwhile, prepare the crudités. Deseed and cut the peppers into 5-cm/2-in strips. Peel the carrots and slice lengthways, cut into fingers about 5 cm/2 in. in length. Slice the celery into small strips of the same length. Break the cauliflower into small florets.

Spoon the taramasalata on to four small plates and arrange the crudités in an attractive pattern on the side of each plate.

Party Tip
For very easy party fare, make several different types of dip with plenty of crudités, crisps and crackers to dunk. Taramasalata makes a tasty dip for such a spread.

Seafood Nests and Saucy Potato Puffs (both recipes overleaf)

SEAFOOD NESTS
SERVES 4
(Illustrated on previous page)

1 kg/2¼ lb potatoes, peeled
salt and freshly ground black pepper
a little milk
grated nutmeg
large knob of butter
Filling
15 g/½ oz butter
15 g/½ oz plain flour
150 ml/¼ pint milk
2 frozen cod steaks, cut into small cubes
100 g/4 oz peeled, cooked prawns
100 g/4 oz crabmeat
2 scallops, chopped (optional)
50 g/2 oz shelled cooked mussels (optional)
150 ml/¼ pint single cream
few drops of lemon juice (optional)
Garnish
chopped parsley
whole cooked prawns

Cook the potatoes in boiling salted water for about 20 minutes or until tender. Drain, then mash them thoroughly until very smooth. Beat in the milk, nutmeg and butter until smooth. Season to taste and leave to cool.

Set the oven at hot (220 C, 425 F, gas 7). When the mixture is cool enough to handle, spoon it into a piping bag fitted with a large star nozzle. Pipe four nests on to a greased ovenproof serving dish. Bake the nests in the heated oven for 10-15 minutes, until lightly browned.

To make the filling, melt the butter in a saucepan, stir in the flour and cook for a minute. Gradually stir in the milk. Bring to the boil, stirring constantly. Add the cod and simmer gently for 2 minutes. Add the prawns, crabmeat and scallops and mussels (if used). Cook gently for 2-3 minutes, then stir in the cream to thin the mixture. Continue to cook gently until all the seafood is cooked. Season to taste, adding a few drops of lemon juice if liked.

Fill the potato nests with the seafood mixture and sprinkle with chopped parsley. Garnish with whole prawns and serve immediately.

SAUCY POTATO PUFFS
SERVES 4
(Illustrated on previous page)

450 g/1 lb potatoes, peeled
salt and freshly ground black pepper
15 g/½ oz butter or margarine
4 tablespoons water
40 g/1½ oz plain flour
1 egg, beaten
50 g/2 oz mature Cheddar cheese, grated
oil for deep frying
Red pepper sauce
2 red peppers
2 onions, chopped
2 cloves garlic, crushed
2 tablespoons chopped parsley
150 ml/¼ pint white wine vinegar
50 g/2 oz soft brown sugar

Cook the potatoes in boiling salted water until just soft – about 20 minutes. Drain well and sieve or thoroughly mash the potatoes. Put the butter or margarine and the water into a small pan, heat until the butter or margarine has melted, then bring to the boil. Quickly tip in the flour, remove from the heat and beat well until the mixture leaves the sides of the pan. Leave to cool until just warm, then gradually beat in the egg. Beat in the cheese, then the mashed potato and season well.

To make the sauce, grill the red peppers until the skins blister, then peel them. Remove the cores and seeds and chop the flesh roughly. Put it into a liquidiser or food processor, with the onion, garlic, parsley and vinegar, then blend until smooth. Put the purée into a pan with the sugar and bring slowly to the boil, stirring frequently. Boil over high heat, stirring constantly, for about 5 minutes, until the sauce is very thick. Add salt to taste and keep warm.

Heat the oil to 190 C/375 F and carefully drop in teaspoonfuls of the potato mixture. Cook for about 2 minutes, until the puffs are crisp and golden. Remove with a slotted spoon and drain on absorbent kitchen paper. Serve at once, with the sauce.

MELON COCKTAIL
SERVES 4

1 small honeydew melon
½ or ¼ water melon
2 tablespoons sweet vermouth
a few sprigs of mint
a little caster sugar

Halve the honeydew melon and scoop out the seeds. Use a melon scoop to remove the flesh in neat balls. Make the water melon flesh into balls, again removing the seeds.

Mix all the melon balls in a bowl and add vermouth with the mint, then sprinkle with a little sugar and chill thoroughly. To serve, spoon the cocktail into glasses and decorate with the sprigs of mint.

Party Tip
Use one or more large whole water melons. Cut off the top, scoop out the flesh leaving the shell whole, then pile the cocktail back in and chill well. This looks very decorative.

GRILLED SPICED GRAPEFRUIT
SERVES 4

2 grapefruit
2 tablespoons dry sherry
¼ teaspoon cinnamon
50 g/2 oz demerara sugar
25 g/1 oz preserved stem ginger, chopped

Cut the grapefruit in half, making 5-mm/¼-in zigzag cuts using a sharp pointed knife. Make sure the cuts reach the centre of the grapefruit. Pull the grapefruit apart carefully. Using a serrated grapefruit knife cut between the membrane of each segment. Cut round the grapefruit to release the segments from the pith. Sprinkle each half with a little of the sherry, cinnamon, sugar and chopped ginger.

Preheat a moderate grill and place the grapefruit cut side uppermost in the grill pan. Cook until the sugar is melted and bubbling but not burning. Serve at once in glass dishes.

Apple Cocktails

APPLE COCKTAILS
SERVES 4

4 small apples
3 tablespoons mayonnaise
1 tablespoon lemon juice
salt and freshly ground black pepper
¼ teaspoon curry powder
8 stuffed green olives, sliced
50-75 g/2-3 oz peeled, cooked prawns or shrimps, halved
1 tablespoon chopped chives
50 g/2 oz Cheddar cheese, finely diced
sprigs of watercress to garnish

Cut a slice off the top of each apple and scoop out the flesh and core, leaving a firm shell inside the peel.

Combine the mayonnaise, lemon juice, seasoning and curry powder. Discard the apple cores and chop the remaining flesh and add to the mayonnaise together with the olives, halved prawns or shrimps, chives and cheese. Mix thoroughly, then spoon back into the apple shells. Arrange on small plates, garnish with the watercress and serve at once.

Scrambled Egg Starter and Lattice Tartlets

SCRAMBLED EGG STARTER

SERVES 6

6 slices toast
25 g/1 oz butter (plus extra
for spreading)
4 eggs
salt and freshly ground black pepper
2 tablespoons single cream or milk
1 (50-g/2-oz) can anchovy fillets,
drained and halved
parsley sprigs to garnish .

Remove the crusts from the toast. Cut each slice in half and then cut into fingers, or triangles. Spread with butter.

Beat the eggs with a little salt and pepper in a bowl. Melt the 25 g/1 oz butter or margarine in a heavy-based pan, pour in the egg mixture and cook over a low heat stirring all the time, until the mixture thickens and the eggs are creamy. Remove the pan from the heat and stir in the cream or milk.

Quickly top the toast with the scrambled eggs and top with the anchovy fillets, arranged in a lattice pattern, and a sprig of parsley.

Party Tip

These savoury fingers can be served cold as well. Beat some grated Cheddar cheese into the hot eggs and add 2 tablespoons chopped chives for extra flavour. Allow to cool, then spread on cold and crisp, well-buttered toast. Add a variety of different garnishes and arrange the 'fingers' on a platter.

LATTICE TARTLETS

MAKES 16

225 g/8 oz plain flour
pinch of salt
100 g/4 oz butter or margarine
about 3 tablespoons cold water
Filling
50 g/2 oz butter or margarine
25 g/1 oz plain flour
300 ml/½ pint milk
salt and freshly ground black pepper
225 g/8 oz button mushrooms, thinly
sliced
parsley sprigs to garnish

Place the flour and salt in a bowl. Rub in the butter or margarine until the mixture resembles fine bread-crumbs. Sprinkle over the water and stir lightly until the mixture begins to bind together to form a dough, adding a little more water if necessary. Knead very lightly. Roll out two-thirds of the pastry thinly. Cut out 16 rounds and use to line patty tins. Prick the pastry all over and chill for 20 minutes.

Melt the butter in a saucepan. Stir in the flour and cook gently for 1 minute. Gradually add the milk stirring all the time. Bring the sauce slowly to the boil, add the mushrooms and seasoning and simmer gently for 2-3 minutes stirring occasionally. Leave the sauce to cool before using to fill the tartlets.

Roll out the reserved pastry and cut it into thin strips. Lay these across the tartlets in a lattice pattern, dampening the edge to keep them in place. Place in a moderate oven (180 C, 350 F, gas 4) for 25-30 minutes. Serve at once, garnished with parsley.

CHEESE PEARS
SERVES 4

*2 ripe pears
2 teaspoons lemon juice
100 g/4 oz cream cheese
1-2 tablespoons single cream
1 teaspoon grated onion
garlic salt
freshly ground black pepper
shredded lettuce to serve
slices of radish to garnish*

Peel the pears and slice them in half lengthwise. Remove the cores with a teaspoon and brush a little lemon juice over surface of the pears to prevent discoloration.

Beat the cream cheese with the cream, grated onion, garlic salt and pepper. Spoon into a piping bag fitted with a star-shaped nozzle. Pipe the mixture into the centre of each pear. Serve on individual plates on a bed of shredded lettuce. Garnish with slices of radish.

MANGO PRAWNS
SERVES 4

*4 mangoes
8 large cooked prawns, peeled
1 red pepper, seeds removed and cut
into strips (optional)
few fresh mint leaves (optional)
8 whole cooked prawns to garnish*
Dressing
*300 ml/½ pint mayonnaise
1 tablespoon horseradish sauce
1 teaspoon caster sugar
freshly ground black pepper*

Slit the mangoes in half lengthwise all the way round the flesh and in as far as the stone. Remove the peel from one half and cut the flesh off the stone. Carefully cut the stone out of the remaining half and remove the flesh, reserving the skin. Cut the flesh in cubes or balls. Cut the prawns into bite-size chunks and combine with the mango flesh.

Make the dressing by mixing the mayonnaise, horseradish sauce, sugar and black pepper together. Mix the prawns and mango with the dressing and pile into the four reserved mango skins. Garnish with strips of red pepper and mint leaves, if used, and the prawns. Serve chilled.

Frosted Grapes (page 31) and Mango Prawns

STUFFED EGGS
SERVES 4

*4 hard-boiled eggs
150 ml/¼ pint mayonnaise
½ teaspoon curry powder
garlic salt
paprika
about ¼ teaspoon ground cinnamon
lettuce leaves to serve
few sprigs of fresh coriander or
parsley to garnish*

Halve the eggs lengthways, scoop out the yolks and mash thoroughly. Add the mayonnaise and curry powder. Season to taste with garlic salt, paprika and cinnamon. Beat thoroughly, then spoon into a piping bag fitted with a small star-shaped nozzle. Pipe a swirl of the curry mixture back into each of the egg whites.

Arrange the lettuce on four small plates and place two egg halves on each. Garnish each filled egg with a sprig of fresh coriander or parsley. Serve with freshly cooked popadums.

Sandwiches & Snacks

For an informal gathering of friends, for brunches, lunches or suppers, ease the work load on yourself and let your guests help themselves to Bumper Sandwiches. Have lots of different types of fresh bread, ready sliced, and plenty of interesting fillings, then encourage people to build up the layers in their own sandwiches.

For a more elegant presentation, make some of the pinwheel sandwiches in this chapter or try some of the tasty snacks which are on offer. Probably easiest of all, and immensely satisfying, are toasted sandwiches. They are ideal for serving as a snack after the cinema or theatre or for light-hearted and impromptu parties.

BUMPER SANDWICHES

For really easy, informal party food, why not make large platters of door-step sandwiches? (Or better still prepare all the ingredients, present them attractively and let your guests help themselves.) Just use really fresh bread, plenty of interesting fillings and build up the layers. Spread softened butter or margarine on the bread (try herb-flavoured butter if you like) and add lashings of mayonnaise, mustard, pickles or relishes if you like. The following ingredients will all lend themselves to this type of sandwich – mix them together as you like. Serve with plenty of well-chilled lager or cider!

Breads: black rye, Granary, wholemeal, crusty white, sesame loaf, milk bread or light rye with caraway.
Fishy Fillings: drained and flaked, canned tuna; mashed sardines (with oil or tomato sauce); flaked or mashed canned salmon; fresh smoked salmon; peeled, cooked prawns or flaked smoked mackerel. Season with freshly ground black pepper and sprinkle with a little lemon juice.
Chicken or Turkey: chopped cooked chicken or turkey, sliced chicken breast or smoked chicken. Season well.
Meats: cooked or smoked ham (try Parma or Bayonne for a very special sandwich), cold roast beef, roast pork, salami or mortadella. Hot, freshly grilled bacon and sausages.
Eggs: scrambled eggs, hard-boiled or fried (good with grilled bacon). Serve with a pinch of nutmeg and plenty of freshly ground black pepper.

Cheese: all types taste good, hard or soft with herbs, garlic or other flavourings.
Vegetables and Salad Ingredients: all fresh and crisp salad ingredients. Cold cooked new potatoes; sliced, cooked beetroot; shredded cabbage and carrots; sliced peppers and avocados.
Fruit: bananas, apples, pears and peaches.
Condiments and Accompaniments: mayonnaise, yogurt-based dressings, a little oil and vinegar, soured cream and tomato ketchup. Chutneys and relishes, mustards of all types and pickles such as onions, cabbage, gherkins and olives.
Garnishes: fresh herbs or watercress.

GARNISHING IDEAS

Vegetable roses Choose vegetables such as radish, tomato and carrot, use a small sharp knife to cut the vegetable skin into spirals. Roll one edge of the spiral over the other to make a cone. Continue in this fashion until a rose-like shape is formed.
Julienne vegetables Choose vegetables such as carrots, celery or peppers. Cut the food into long strips about 5-cm/2-in wide, then into fine strips.
Spring onion curls Cut each spring onion into 5-cm/2-in lengths. Shred the ends of the spring onions, then soak them in iced water.
To use a canelling knife A canelling knife is used to pare the skin of fruit or vegetables and can also be used to cut the grooves or channels lengthways down courgettes, carrots and cucumber.

TOASTED SANDWICHES

Toasted sandwiches make deliciously satisfying hot snacks or can easily replace a meal. If you can borrow a couple of extra sandwich toasters from friends, then why not invite lots of people in for a toasted sandwich party? Each of the following fillings will make two sandwiches for which you will need 4 bread slices and some butter or margarine.

Spread four slices of bread with butter or margarine. Mix together one of the suggested fillings and use to sandwich the bread together. Press the slices of bread together firmly. Place each sandwich directly between the cooking plates of a contact grill or sandwich maker and cook for 3 minutes or until the outside of the bread is crisp and golden. Serve immediately.

A Bumper Sandwich

Chicken
100 g/4 oz cooked chicken, diced
50 g/2 oz full fat soft cheese, diced
salt and freshly ground black pepper

Prawn and Ham
2 thin slices cooked ham
100 g/4 oz peeled, cooked prawns
salt and freshly ground black pepper

Turkey and Cranberry
25 g/1 oz softened butter
1 tablespoon cranberry sauce
100 g/4 oz cooked turkey, diced
salt and freshly ground black pepper

Apple and Blue Cheese
1 dessert apple, peeled, cored and sliced
100 g/4 oz Stilton cheese, sliced

Garlic Sausage and Mushroom Cream
25 g/1 oz butter or margarine
4 slices garlic sausage
50 g/2 oz button mushrooms, chopped
50 g/2 oz full fat soft cheese, diced

Chicken and Corn
100 g/4 oz cooked chicken, diced
4 tablespoons canned sweetcorn kernels
50 g/2 oz full fat soft cheese

Curried Chicken
25 g/1 oz peanut butter
100 g/4 oz cooked chicken, chopped
1 teaspoon concentrated curry paste
50 g/2 oz full fat soft cheese

Cottage Cheese and Bacon
25 g/1 oz butter or margarine
2 rindless lean bacon rashers, halved
50 g/2 oz cottage cheese

Sage Derby and Pear
25 g/1 oz butter
50 g/2 oz Derby cheese, grated
1 small pear, peeled, cored and sliced

Salmon Relish
1 (53-g/1⅞-oz) pot salmon pâté
1 tablespoon sweetcorn relish
4 spring onions, finely chopped
generous pinch of nutmeg

Devilled Crab
1 (53-g/2-oz) pot crab spread
1 teaspoon concentrated tomato purée
½ teaspoon French mustard
50 g/2 oz cheese, grated
dash of Worcestershire sauce

PARTY TIME SANDWICH SHAPES
MAKES ABOUT 50

1 large sliced wholemeal loaf
100 g/4 oz softened butter or margarine
Cream Cheese Filling
100 g/4 oz cream cheese
1 tablespoon chopped parsley or chives
salt and freshly ground black pepper
Egg Filling
2 hard-boiled eggs, mashed
2-3 tablespoons thick mayonnaise
salt and freshly ground black pepper
Pâté and Cucumber Filling
100 g/4 oz smooth pâté
¼ cucumber, thinly sliced
watercress or mustard and cress to garnish

Remove the crusts from the bread and spread with the butter or margarine.

Mix together the ingredients for the chosen filling. Spread the filling on half the buttered slices and sandwich together with the remaining slices. Cut the sandwiches either into fingers, small triangles or use shaped cutters (animal-shaped cutters make great sandwiches for a children's party). Arrange the sandwiches attractively on a plate, (if using animal-shaped cutters, make them stand upright).

Garnish the plate with watercress or mustard and cress.

Variations
Try the following filling on the sandwiches:
Curried Egg Filling Mash 2 hard-boiled eggs with 3 tablespoons mayonnaise and ¼-½ teaspoon curry paste. Add 1 finely chopped spring onion and seasoning to taste.
Tuna and Tomato Filling Drain and mash 1 (200-g/7-oz) can tuna. Mix in 2 finely chopped peeled tomatoes, 2 tablespoons finely chopped parsley and 2 tablespoons lemon juice. Season to taste.
Garnishing ideas Top the tiny sandwich shapes with quartered slices of lemon, cucumber and tomato. Add tiny sprigs of watercress or parsley if you like.
Party Tip
Sandwich shapes are great for children's parties. They are more likely to prefer the egg and cream cheese fillings to the pâté and cucumber one.

SMOKED SALMON ROLLS
MAKES 12-15

1 small wholemeal loaf
100 g/4 oz butter or margarine
100 g/4 oz smoked salmon pieces
freshly ground black pepper
lemon juice
Garnish
lemon twists
parsley sprigs

Cut the crusts from the top, bottom, both ends and one side of the loaf. Lay the loaf on a bread board with the remaining crust on one side. Holding the crusted side in one hand, lightly spread the opposite side with butter or margarine. Slice off the buttered side as thinly as possible, cutting along the length of the loaf. Continue in this way until the loaf is finished. Discard the crust.

Place a piece of smoked salmon on each slice of bread, leaving a 1-cm/½-in border along one short side and narrow borders around the other sides. Sprinkle with black pepper and lemon juice. Roll up neatly from the 1-cm/½-in border, spreading the final edge with a little extra butter or margarine if it does not stick.

Trim the rolls and cut into two or three equal pieces. Garnish with twists of lemon and parsley.

PÂTÉ PINWHEELS
MAKES ABOUT 50

1 large uncut white sandwich loaf
225 g/8 oz butter or margarine, softened
225 g/8 oz smooth pâté
Garnish
parsley sprigs
cherry tomatoes, quartered

Cut the crusts from the top, bottom, both ends and one side of the loaf. Holding the remaining crusted side in one hand, spread the opposite side thinly with the butter or margarine and pâté. Slice thinly along the length of the bread. Roll up tightly from the short end along the length of the slice. Continue in this way until all the bread is used up.

Trim the ends and cut each roll into five equal slices like a Swiss roll. Serve garnished with parsley and quarters of cherry tomato.

PIZZA DISCS
MAKES 10

*1 medium onion, chopped
1 clove garlic, crushed
25 g/1 oz butter or margarine
1 (396-g/14-oz) can tomatoes
1 teaspoon dried oregano
salt and freshly ground black pepper
1 tablespoon cornflour
10 rusks or toast rounds
100 g/4 oz Cheddar or Gruyère cheese,
grated
1 (50-g/2-oz) can anchovies, drained
sprigs of watercress to garnish*

Place the onion, garlic and butter or margarine in a saucepan and cook gently for 5 minutes until soft and transparent. Drain the tomatoes and add to the pan with the dried herbs and seasoning. Stir well and simmer for 10-15 minutes until thickened. Blend the cornflour with a little cold water, stir into the tomatoes and cook, stirring, until the cornflour has thickened.

Set the oven at moderately hot (200 C, 400 F, gas 6).

Place the rusks on a baking sheet and divide the sauce between the biscuits spreading the mixture evenly. Top each with grated cheese. Cut the anchovy fillets in half lengthways and arrange these in a criss-cross pattern on top of each biscuit.

Place in the heated oven for 8-10 minutes to heat through and melt the cheese. Garnish with watercress.
Party Tip
Serve these piping hot with a green salad or coleslaw. If you are preparing dozens of pizza discs, make them in advance, ready on trays to be heated in a hurry at the last minute.

AVOCADO PINWHEELS
MAKES ABOUT 50

Use the following avocado mixture as an alternative filling for the Pâté Pinwheels, substituting wholemeal bread for the white, if liked.

*2 avocados
100 g/4 oz cream or curd cheese
1 teaspoon lemon juice
½ small onion, grated
salt and freshly ground black pepper*

Halve, stone and peel the avocados. Place the avocados and the remaining ingredients in the liquidiser, and blend until smooth.

Pizza Discs

DANISH SARDINE SANDWICHES
MAKES 1

*1 large slice bread
softened butter or margarine for spreading
1 lettuce leaf
1 slice cheese (Tilsit, Edam,
Gruyère, Farmhouse Cheddar or
similar hard cheese)
2 canned sardines, drained
1 tomato, sliced
¼ onion, diced
salt and freshly ground black pepper*

Remove the crusts from the bread and cut into a neat square. Spread the butter or margarine over the bread.

Place the lettuce on the bread. Top with the cheese. Lay the sardines diagonally across the cheese and arrange the sliced tomato on top. Sprinkle the diced onion on the tomato and season to taste. Serve at once.

LUXURY CHICKEN SANDWICH
MAKES 1

2-3 lettuce leaves
1 large, fairly thick slice brown bread
butter or margarine for spreading
100 g/4 oz cooked chicken breast
1 canned peach half, drained
1 tablespoon mayonnaise
chopped parsley

Wash the lettuce and dry thoroughly. Spread the bread with the butter or margarine. Cut the bread in half diagonally. Place the lettuce on top of each half. Skin the chicken breast, slice thinly and arrange in layers on the lettuce. Cut the peach half into equal slices, and place in a fan-shape on the chicken. Spoon the mayonnaise into a piping bag fitted with a star-shaped nozzle and pipe swirls on to the peaches. Sprinkle with chopped parsley.

PARTY CRACKERS
MAKES 24

225 g/8 oz curd cheese
3 tablespoons single cream
1 teaspoon lemon juice
½ teaspoon salt
generous pinch of cayenne
generous pinch of sugar
½ small onion, grated
2 tablespoons chopped fresh mixed herbs (chervil, chives, parsley, dill) or 2 teaspoons dried mixed herbs
24 cheese biscuits
Garnish
1 large carrot
dill or parsley sprigs

Beat the curd cheese with the cream, lemon juice, salt, cayenne and sugar until smooth. Fold the grated onion into the cheese mixture together with the mixed herbs. Transfer the mixture to a piping bag fitted with a star-shaped nozzle and pipe on to the biscuits.

Blanch the carrot in boiling water for 1-2 minutes. Cut into 24 slices. Using a patterned pastry cutter or knife, shape the carrot slices into flower shapes. Garnish each biscuit with a slice of carrot and a parsley or dill sprig.

SPICY CHEESE TWISTS
MAKES ABOUT 15

1 (368-g/13-oz) packet frozen puff pastry, thawed
1 egg
1 tablespoon milk
½ teaspoon ground cloves
25 g/1 oz butter
4 tablespoons fresh wholemeal breadcrumbs
3 tablespoons single cream
50 g/2 oz mature Cheddar cheese, grated
2 drops Worcestershire sauce
1 teaspoon ground coriander
½ teaspoon grated nutmeg
3 tablespoons water

Set the oven at moderately hot (200 C, 400 F, gas 6). Roll the pastry out to about 5-mm/¼-in thick on a floured surface. Brush with a mixture of the egg, milk and cloves, beaten together. Melt the butter and stir in the breadcrumbs, cream, cheese, Worcestershire sauce, coriander, nutmeg and water. Spread evenly over the pastry, then cut into 2.5-cm/1-in wide strips. Press two strips together, with the pastry and filling forming alternate layers. Twist the double-thick strip. Repeat with the remaining strips. Place the strips on a greased baking tray and bake in the heated oven for 25 minutes. Serve warm or cold.

COTTAGE HAM CORNETS
MAKES 8

8 slices roast ham
225 g/8 oz cottage cheese with prawns or pineapple
1 small onion, finely chopped
1 tablespoon chopped parsley
salt and freshly ground black pepper
parsley sprigs to garnish

Place the slices of ham individually on a kitchen board. Mix together the cottage cheese, onion and parsley. Season with salt and pepper. Spread half of each slice of ham with all but two tablespoons of the mixture, and roll up the slices into cones. With a teaspoon, fill the larger opening of each roll with the remaining filling and arrange the rolls on a flat dish with the parsley.

HAM AND ASPARAGUS ROLLS

SERVES 6

small bundle asparagus, trimmed or
1 (340-g/12-oz) can asparagus spears
salt
150 ml/¼ pint thick mayonnaise
1-2 cloves garlic, crushed
grated rind of 1 lemon
1-2 tablespoons single cream
6 slices cooked ham
paprika to garnish

Cook the asparagus, if using fresh, in salted water until just tender, drain and cool. If using canned asparagus, drain well. Combine the mayonnaise with garlic and lemon rind to taste and add sufficient single cream to give a coating consistency.

Divide the asparagus between the slices of ham and roll up. Put the ham rolls on a serving dish or six small plates. Spoon the mayonnaise mixture over the ham and sprinkle with paprika. Serve with brown bread and butter.

Ham and Asparagus Rolls

YORK SAVOURIES

MAKES 32

350 g/12 oz mature Cheddar cheese
1 (368-g/13-oz) packet frozen puff pastry,
thawed
225 g/8 oz sliced ham
beaten egg or milk to glaze

Set the oven at hot (230 C, 450 F, gas 8).

Thinly slice 275 g/10 oz of the cheese and finely grate the remaining 50 g/2 oz.

Roll out the pastry to a 40-cm/16-in square. Cut the square into four 40 x 10-cm/16 x 4-in rectangles. On two of the rectangles of pastry place a layer of sliced cheese and ham and place the other two rectangles on top. Brush with beaten egg or milk and sprinkle with the grated cheese. Cut the rectangles into 32 (2.5 x 10-cm/1 x 4-in) fingers. Alternatively cut them into diamond shapes, small squares or decorative shapes (using cutters). Place on a dampened baking tray and bake in the heated oven for 5-7 minutes until puffed and golden brown. Cool on a wire rack, serve warm or cold.

Simple Finger Food

Preparing lots of fiddly canapés and tit-bits can take as long as making a buffet meal. So if you are having a drinks party but want to keep the food preparation to a minimum, then take a look at the ideas in this chapter. Savoury pastries and biscuits can be made the day before the party, similarly, cocktail croquettes can be prepared and shaped a day in advance ready for frying a few hours before the event. Assemble cocktail-stick snacks on the same day, keeping them covered and refrigerated until the last minute.

Arrange the food as attractively as possible on plates or dishes which can be handed round. Add colourful garnishes and make a decorative display of napkins on one corner of the table so that people can take one if they like. For a change make a few sweet snacks in addition to the savouries, they are good to serve with coffee just before everyone leaves if not earlier on for those who favour sweet foods.

SIMPLE SAVOURIES
MAKES 30

Gherkins and ham
10 thin slices ham
freshly ground black pepper
10 cocktail gherkins
Dates and cream cheese
10 dates
2 tablespoons single cream
75 g/3 oz full fat cream cheese
½ teaspoon finely chopped dill or parsley
Olives and bacon
10 thin slices streaky bacon
10 stuffed olives

Sprinkle the ham with the pepper. Wrap each gherkin in a slice of ham and secure with a cocktail stick.

Slice the dates open lengthways and remove the stones. Beat the cream and cream cheese together until smooth. Mix in the herbs. Transfer the mixture to a piping bag fitted with a small star-shaped nozzle and pipe into the dates. Keep the stuffed dates in a cool place until you are ready to serve them.

Fry the bacon until cooked on both sides but still soft. Drain for a few minutes on absorbent kitchen paper. Wrap a stuffed olive in each slice of bacon, securing with a wooden cocktail stick. Return the bacon rolls to the pan and fry in hot fat until crisp, turning occasionally.

SAVOURY COCKTAIL STICKS
SERVES 4

450 g/1 lb Edam cheese
50 g/2 oz thinly sliced salami
24 stuffed olives
4 cherry tomatoes
parsley sprigs to garnish

Cut the cheese into small cubes. Roll up the salami slices. Thread each salami roll on to a cocktail stick with an olive, a small parsley sprig and a cheese cube.

Wash, dry and cut the tomatoes into quarters. Thread the tomato quarters on to cocktail sticks, each with an olive and a cheese cube. Thread the remaining cheese cubes on to sticks, interspersed with olives, and garnish with parsley sprigs.

Party Tip
If you're short on table space or want to position these snacks on small tables round the room, then stick them into grapefruit and place these on small plates.

Creamy Herb Bread (page 29)

BANANA BACON SAVOURIES

MAKES 30

1 (212-g/7½-oz) packet frozen puff pastry,
thawed
5 bananas
juice of 1 lemon
350 g/12 oz rindless lean bacon
beaten egg or milk to glaze

Set the oven at hot (230 C, 450 F, gas 8). Roll the pastry out to a rectangle measuring 45 x 60 cm/18 x 24 in. Trim the edges and cut into strips measuring approximately 3.5 x 45 cm/1½ x 18 in. Cut the strips in half so that they measure 23 cm/9 in. in length.

Cut each banana into six pieces and dip in the lemon juice. Wrap each piece of banana in half a rasher of bacon and wrap in a strip of pastry, dampening the end with water to seal. Placed on dampened baking trays and brush with a little beaten egg or milk. Bake in the heated oven for 10-15 minutes. Serve warm or cold.

Cheese Biscuits (opposite) and Puff Pastry Pinwheels;
Savoury Tartlets (page 40) and Banana Bacon Savouries

PUFF PASTRY PINWHEELS

MAKES 36

1 (215-g/7½-oz) packet frozen puff pastry,
thawed
2 (120-g/4¼-oz) cans sardines in oil
100 g/4 oz full fat soft cheese
1 teaspoon dried chives
grated rind and juice of 1 lemon

Set the oven at moderately hot (200 C, 400 F, gas 6). Grease a baking tray. Roll the pastry out on a lightly floured surface to an oblong measuring 35 x 18 cm/14 x 7 in. Mash the sardines with their oil, then beat in the remaining ingredients and spread evenly over the pastry. Roll up from the long side to give a 35-cm/14-in long roll. Chill thoroughly. Slice the roll vertically like a Swiss roll into 36 slices. Place well apart on the baking tray and bake in the heated oven for 10-15 minutes.

Party Tip

Fill and roll up the pastry a day in advance, then chill it until a few hours before the party. Slice and cook as above so that the pinwheels will be crisp and fresh.

CREAMY HERB BREAD
SERVES 8-10

(Illustrated on page 27)

225 g/8 oz full-fat soft cheese
salt and freshly ground black pepper
large bunch of mixed fresh herbs,
for example parsley, thyme, rosemary,
mint, basil, marjoram and dill
1 French loaf

Cream the cheese with seasoning to taste. Wash, trim and chop the herbs. Use as many different herbs as you can find, but take care not to overpower the delicate flavours with strong herbs like mint or rosemary which should be used in smaller quantities. Beat the herbs into the cheese.

Cut the loaf into slices, leaving them all attached at the base. Spread the cream cheese mixture between the slices, then press the bread back together. Wrap the loaf in cooking foil (you may have to cut the bread in half so that it fits in the oven), sealing the edges together well.

Put the bread in a moderately hot oven (200 C, 400 F, gas 6) for about 20-25 minutes or until hot and crisp. Separate the slices and serve at once.

Variations
Lemon Parsley Bread Use chopped parsley and the grated rind of 1 lemon instead of the mixed herbs. Add 1-2 tablespoons lemon juice.
Walnut and Garlic Bread Beat 50 g/2 oz finely chopped walnuts and 1 crushed clove garlic into the cream cheese instead of the herbs.

CHEESE BISCUITS
MAKES 35

225 g/8 oz plain flour
100 g/4 oz margarine
2 tablespoons cold water
100 g/4 oz mature Cheddar cheese,
finely grated
1 teaspoon dry mustard
2 teaspoons caraway seeds
beaten egg or milk to glaze
Topping
100 g/4 oz cream cheese
50 g/2 oz stuffed green olives, sliced

Set the oven at moderately hot (200 C, 400 F, gas 6). Grease two baking trays. Make the pastry following the instruction for Savoury Tartlets (page 40) but adding the grated cheese, mustard and caraway seeds to the rubbed-in dry ingredients. Roll out the pastry to 5-mm/¼-in thickness. Use a 3.5-cm/1½-in pastry cutter to cut out the biscuits. Place on the baking trays, brush with a little beaten egg or milk and bake in the heated oven for 10-15 minutes. Cool on a wire rack.

Fit a piping bag with a small star nozzle and fill with the cream cheese. Pipe a little cream cheese on top of each biscuit and top with a slice of olive.

CHICKEN AND MUSHROOM CROQUETTES
SERVES 6-8

450 g/1 lb mushrooms
50 g/2 oz butter or margarine
100 g/4 oz plain flour
150 ml/¼ pint milk
2 eggs plus 2 egg yolks
575 g/1¼ lb boneless chicken meat
100 g/4 oz ham, finely chopped
2 tablespoons chopped parsley
3 tablespoons Madeira
salt and freshly ground black pepper
100 g/4 oz dried breadcrumbs
oil for deep frying

Clean the mushrooms and cut off the tips of the stalks. Melt half the butter or margarine in a saucepan, sprinkle on 25 g/1 oz flour and stir over the heat until golden. Gradually add the milk and simmer the sauce for 10 minutes, stirring continuously. Leave the sauce to cool slightly, then stir in the two egg yolks.

Lightly beat the two remaining eggs. Skin and trim the chicken and mince twice through the finest blade of the mincer. Mix the mince with the sauce, ham, parsley, 25 g/1 oz flour, the remaining butter, the Madeira and the salt and pepper, and knead to form a smooth dough. Wet your hands and surround each mushroom with a ball of the mixture, lightly pressing the meat together. Coat the balls with the remaining flour, then the beaten egg and finally the breadcrumbs. Heat the oil for deep frying to 180 C/350 F. Fry the croquettes for 6-8 minutes until brown and crispy. Drain on absorbent kitchen paper and leave to cool.

Party Tip
Croquettes such as these are ideal for taking on picnic parties. Once cooked they are easily eaten with the fingers and taste good with simple salad ingredients.

WALNUT PAIRS
MAKES ABOUT 24

*75 g/3 oz cream cheese
onion salt
paprika
48 walnut halves (about 100 g/4 oz)*

Beat the cheese until soft and season to taste with onion salt and paprika. Spread or pipe the cheese onto the walnut halves and sandwich together.

FROSTED GRAPES
SERVES 6

*1 kg/2¼ lb seedless grapes
2 egg whites, lightly beaten
175 g/6 oz icing sugar, sifted*

Wash the grapes thoroughly and drain. Cut the stems to make small clusters of grapes. Dip each cluster of grapes into the beaten egg white and dust generously with icing sugar. Place on a baking tray and put in the freezer or ice-making compartment of a refrigerator for 30 minutes, then refrigerate until ready to serve.

Party Tip
A large glass platter of frosted grapes makes an elegant addition to a simple buffet of cheese, cold meats and wine.

HAZELNUT TRUFFLES
MAKES ABOUT 20

*50 g/2 oz hazelnuts
50 g/2 oz unsalted butter
100 g/4 oz porridge oats
100 g/4 oz caster sugar
2-3 tablespoons melted chocolate or
cocoa powder
rum essence
3-4 tablespoons black coffee*

Rub the skins off the nuts. Beat the butter until soft and work in the oats, sugar and chocolate or cocoa powder until well blended. Add a few drops of rum essence and enough coffee to bind the mixture without making it sticky.

Leave the mixture in a cool place to firm slightly, then divide into small pieces and shape into round balls. Set a hazelnut on top of each ball and press down lightly. Alternatively, chop the nuts finely and use to coat the balls. Place in sweet cases and serve.

NUT AND SULTANA BARS
MAKES 12 BARS

*100 g/4 oz digestive biscuits
50 g/2 oz plain sweet biscuits
75 g/3 oz sultanas
75 g/3 oz walnuts, chopped
2 tablespoons golden syrup
75 g/3 oz butter
50 g/2 oz plain chocolate*

Grease a shallow 18-cm/7-in square tin. Put all the biscuits in a polythene bag and crush with a rolling pin. Put into a bowl and mix in the sultanas and walnuts.

Place the golden syrup, butter and chocolate in a small bowl over a pan of simmering water and stir until the mixture has melted and is well combined. Pour on to the biscuit, fruit and nut mixture and mix well to combine. Spoon into the prepared tin and smooth with a palette knife. Chill until set. Use a hot wet knife to cut into bars before serving.

Nut and Sultana Bars, Hazelnut Truffles and Walnut Pairs

Pies & Pastries

Summer offers the opportunity to eat outside and a great way to celebrate a special occasion is to have a picnic party. Pies, flans and pasties can be easily transported to look as good when they arrive as they did when they left the kitchen.

For festive winter celebrations you can always keep the event very simple and serve lots of hot mince pies with warming mulled wine. The versatile pastry dishes in this chapter will suit every occasion, from the most informal meals to the most elaborate parties.

CHICKEN AND HAM PIE
SERVES 4-6

100-150 g/4-5 oz cooked chicken, chopped
50 g/2 oz cooked ham, diced
150 g/5 oz Lancashire cheese, diced
50 g/2 oz mushrooms, chopped
1 small onion, finely chopped
1 tablespoon chopped parsley
salt and freshly ground black pepper
1 egg, beaten
1 (212-g/7½-oz) packet puff pastry, beaten egg to glaze
Garnish
tomato quarters
sprigs of watercress

Mix together the chicken, ham, cheese, mushrooms, onion and parsley. Season to taste. Stir the beaten egg into the mixture. Roll the pastry thinly into a rectangle 39 × 25-cm/15 × 10-in. Cut out a 25-cm/10-in square. Place on a baking tray. Pile the filling in the centre. Fold the corners of the square to the centre and seal the edges with beaten egg. Brush all over the pie evenly with egg. Use the remaining pastry to decorate the pie. Glaze the decorations with the egg and arrange on the pie. Open the outer corners of the envelope slightly to allow steam to escape during cooking.

Set the oven at hot (220 C, 425 F, gas 7). Bake in the heated oven for 25 minutes until well risen and golden brown. Serve hot or cold and garnish with tomato quarters and fresh watercress.

CORNISH PASTIES
MAKES 6

Pastry
450 g/1 lb plain flour
¼ teaspoon salt
225 g/8 oz margarine
about 3 tablespoons cold water
Filling
350 g/12 oz potato
225 g/8 oz swede
2 large onions, finely chopped
450 g/1 lb beef skirt or chuck steak
salt and freshly ground black pepper
beaten egg to glaze

Make the shortcrust following the instructions on page 40. Roll out the pastry and cut into six rounds about 15 cm/6 in. in diameter. Cut the potato and swede into small dice and mix with the finely chopped onion. Finely chop the meat and stir into the vegetable mixture. Season well with salt and pepper. Divide the filling between the pastry rounds, brush the edges with beaten egg and bring up opposite sides to meet over the filling. Seal well together and flute the edges. Brush with beaten egg and cut a small steam vent in the top. Place on a baking tray and bake in a moderate oven (180 C, 350 F, gas 4) for about 50 minutes, until the pasties are golden brown.

Chicken and Ham Pie

RAISED TURKEY PIE

S E R V E S   8 - 1 0

Filling
25 g/1 oz butter
1 large onion, finely chopped
grated rind of 2 lemons
3 tablespoons chopped parsley
salt and freshly ground black pepper
900 g/2 lb turkey meat
Hot water crust pastry
500 g/18 oz plain flour
½ teaspoon salt
175 g/6 oz lard
5-6 tablespoons water
5-6 tablespoons milk
To finish
beaten egg or milk to glaze
15 g/½ oz powdered aspic
300 ml/½ pint boiling water
Garnish
1 lemon, sliced
small sprigs of watercress

Melt the butter, add the onion and cook until soft but not browned. Stir in the lemon rind and parsley and season generously. Thinly slice the turkey.

Place the flour and salt in a bowl. Place the lard, water and milk in a saucepan and heat gently until the lard melts. Bring to the boil, then pour on to the flour and mix in quickly. Keep one-third of the pastry hot in a basin over a saucepan of boiling water. Using warm hands and working quickly, roll out the remaining pastry to give an oval shape slightly larger than the top of a 23-cm/9-in raised pie mould. Dust the inside of the mould with flour and place the pastry on top. Keeping the edge of pastry around the inside of the tin, gently mould the pastry down the sides and base to cover the inside completely and evenly.

Layer the turkey and onion mixture in the pie. Dampen the pastry rim with water, cover with the pastry lid, dampen the edges with water and press together well to seal. Trim away any excess pastry. Cut a hole in the top to allow any steam to escape and use any pastry trimmings to decorate the pie. Brush with beaten egg or milk and bake in a moderately hot oven (200 C, 400 F, gas 6) for 40 minutes.

Remove the sides of the mould and brush the sides of the pie with a little beaten egg or milk. Bake in a moderate oven (180 C, 350 F, gas 4) for a further 10 minutes. Cover the top of the pie with a piece of

Raised Turkey Pie, Picnic Pie and Almond Apple Squares (page 41)

cooking foil if it becomes too brown during cooking.

When the pie has cooled, dissolve the aspic in the boiling water, cool slightly, then pour carefully into the pie through the hole in the top. Leave in a cool place until set. Serve garnished with lemon slices and small sprigs of watercress.

Party Tip
Raised pies are superb as the main feature of summer luncheon parties, served with plenty of salads. They are quite filling, so go a long way.

PICNIC PIE

S E R V E S   8 - 1 0

Filling
225 g/8 oz minced pork
225 g/8 oz minced beef
1 tablespoon powdered sage
25 g/1 oz butter
2 cloves garlic, crushed
1 large onion, chopped
1 large green pepper, deseeded and chopped
4 hard-boiled eggs
salt and freshly ground black pepper
Hot water crust pastry
350 g/12 oz plain flour
½ teaspoon salt
100 g/4 oz lard
4 tablespoons water
4 tablespoons milk
beaten egg or milk to glaze

Mix the pork and beef with the sage. Melt the butter in a pan, add the garlic and onion and cook for a few minutes until the onion is just soft. Add the green pepper and stir into the meat mixture. Season generously.

Make the pastry according to the instructions opposite and use two-thirds to line a 1-kg/2¼-lb loaf tin. Place half the meat in the bottom of the tin and arrange the whole eggs on top. Cover with the remaining meat and roll out the reserved pastry to form a lid. Place the lid on the pie, trim and seal the dampened edges. Use any pastry trimmings to decorate the pie. Brush with beaten egg or milk and bake in a moderate oven (180 C, 350 F, gas 4) for 2½-3 hours until well browned. Allow to cool in the tin, then carefully turn out while the pie is still warm.

QUICHE LORRAINE
SERVES 4 - 6

Pastry
225 g/8 oz plain flour
pinch of salt
100 g/4 oz margarine
about 3 tablespoons cold water
Filling
50 g/2 oz butter
1 large onion, finely chopped
3 eggs
300 ml/½ pint single cream or milk
salt and freshly ground black pepper
225 g/8 oz rindless streaky bacon,
coarsely chopped
100 g/4 oz Gruyère or mature Cheddar
cheese, thinly sliced
2 teaspoons chopped mixed fresh herbs
Garnish
1-2 tomatoes, sliced
parsley sprigs

Make the shortcrust pastry according to the instructions on page 40 and use to line a 23-cm/9-in flan dish. Prick the base of the flan all over with a fork and line with foil or greaseproof paper. Weight the paper with dried beans and bake 'blind' in a moderately hot oven (200 C, 400 F, gas 6) for 15 minutes. Remove the paper and beans and continue to cook for a further 5 minutes.

Meanwhile prepare the filling. Melt the butter in a frying pan, add the onion and cook until the onion is soft but not browned. Beat the eggs together and stir in the cream or milk. Season well. Place the onion and bacon in the bottom of the flan and arrange the cheese and herbs on top. Pour over the egg and cream mixture and bake in a moderate oven (180 C, 350 F, gas 4) for 35-40 minutes until set and golden brown. Garnish with sliced tomatoes and a few sprigs of parsley.

PEPPERONI PIZZA
SERVES 6

Base
¼ teaspoon sugar
150 ml/¼ pint warm water
1½ teaspoons dried yeast
225 g/8 oz plain flour
pinch of salt
15 g/½ oz butter or margarine
Topping
1 tablespoon oil
1 onion, chopped
1 (396-g/14-oz) can chopped tomatoes
1 clove garlic, crushed
2 teaspoons dried oregano
salt and freshly ground black pepper
100 g/4 oz mozzarella or Cheddar
cheese, thinly sliced (optional)
1 (100-g/4-oz) piece pepperoni
sausage, sliced

To make the dough, dissolve the sugar in the water and sprinkle the yeast on top. Leave in a warm place for 10 minutes or until frothy. Sift the flour and salt into a bowl and rub in the butter or margarine. Mix to a dough with the yeast liquid. Knead for about 10 minutes or until smooth. Put into an oiled bowl, cover with greased cling film and leave until doubled in size. Knead the dough again for 5 minutes or until smooth. Roll the dough out on a lightly-floured surface to a circle 5-mm/¼-in thick and shape into a 20-cm/8-in circle. Place on a greased baking tray.

To make the topping, heat the oil and fry the onion gently until soft, but not browned. Add the tomatoes, garlic and oregano and season lightly with salt and pepper. Cook, uncovered, until very thick – about 20 minutes. .

Set the oven at hot (220 C, 425 F, gas 7). Spread the topping evenly over the dough. Arrange the slices of cheese on top, if using, and then the pepperoni. Bake in the heated oven for 25 minutes. Cut into wedges and serve immediately.

KIPPER FLAN

S E R V E S   4 - 6

Pastry
175 g/6 oz wholemeal flour
pinch of salt
75 g/3 oz butter or margarine
2-3 tablespoons cold water
Filling
225 g/8 oz kipper fillets, cooked
175 g/6 oz mashed potato
25 g/1 oz butter, softened
1 egg, beaten
4 tablespoons single cream
freshly ground black pepper
75 g/3 oz Cheddar cheese, grated
1 (50-g/2-oz) can anchovy fillets,
drained

To make the pastry, sift the flour and salt into a mixing bowl and rub in the butter or margarine with your fingertips until the mixture resembles fine bread-crumbs. Stir in enough water to make a soft but not sticky dough. Wrap the dough in greaseproof paper and chill it in the refrigerator for 20 minutes while you make the filling. Set the oven at moderately hot (190 C, 375 F, gas 5).

Peperoni Pizza (opposite) and Kipper Flan

To make the filling, mash together the kipper fillets and potato until smooth. Beat in the butter, egg and cream and season to taste with black pepper.

Roll out the chilled dough on a lightly-floured surface and use it to line a 23-cm/9-in flan dish. Spoon in the filling and top with the cheese. Bake in the heated oven for 20-25 minutes, or until lightly browned and set. Before serving, cut the anchovy fillets in half lengthways, then cut each into two or three pieces. Arrange the pieces round the edge of the flan in a decorative pattern. Serve warm, with a mixed salad.

LAMB PIES

M A K E S 6

Filling
2 tablespoons oil
1 small onion, finely chopped
1 small carrot, diced
1 small potato, diced
450 g/1 lb lean lamb, finely diced
4 tablespoons chicken stock
salt and freshly ground black pepper

Hot water crust pastry
350 g/12 oz plain flour
½ teaspoon salt
100 g/4 oz lard
4 tablespoons water
4 tablespoons milk
beaten egg or milk to glaze

Grease a baking tray. Heat the oil in a frying pan and gently sauté the onion until soft but not browned. Add the carrot, potato and lamb and continue to cook until the meat is lightly browned. Add the stock and season well. Leave until cool.

Make the pastry according to the recipe instructions (page 40) and divide into six equal portions. Reserve one-third of each portion and roll the remainder to a

Lamb Pies and Samosas (opposite)

14-cm/5½-in round. Cover the upturned bases of six jam jars with aluminium cooking foil or cling film and mould a circle of pastry round each. Tie a double band of greaseproof paper round the pastry and leave in a cool place until set. Carefully remove the pastry cases from the jam jars leaving the greaseproof band round the outside. Remove the foil or cling film and place each pie on the baking tray. Divide the filling between the pies and roll out the reserve pastry to make lids. Dampen the pastry rims with water. Place the lids on top of the pies sealing the edges well. Make a small hole in the top of each pie to allow any steam to escape and brush with a little beaten egg or milk. Bake in a moderately hot oven (200 C, 400 F, gas 6) for 20 minutes.

Remove the greaseproof bands and glaze the sides of the pies with beaten egg or milk. Continue cooking for a further 15-20 minutes. Serve hot or cold.

SAMOSAS
MAKES 12

Filling
175 g/6 oz minced lamb
1 small onion, finely chopped
1 teaspoon ground cumin
1 teaspoon ground coriander
¼ teaspoon mustard seeds (optional)
1 tablespoon grated root ginger
1 large clove garlic, crushed
salt and freshly ground black pepper
1 small carrot, par-boiled and diced
1 small potato, par-boiled and diced
50 g/2 oz frozen peas
Pastry
225 g/8 oz plain flour
pinch of salt
100 g/4 oz margarine
about 3 tablespoons cold water
1 egg, lightly beaten
oil for deep frying

Place the lamb in a frying pan with the onion and cook gently until the fat runs. Add the cumin, coriander, mustard seeds if used, ginger and garlic and continue to cook until the onion is soft. Season generously, then stir in the vegetables.

Make the pastry according to the instructions on page 40, adding the egg with the water to form a soft dough. Knead lightly until smooth, then divide into 12 equal portions. Roll each piece of dough out to give a 10-cm/4-in square. Place some of the filling on the pastry and dampen the edges with water. Fold two opposite corners together and seal the edges to form a triangular pasty.

Deep fry the samosas, a few at a time, until golden brown, about 3-5 minutes. Drain on absorbent kitchen paper and serve hot.

VOLS-AU-VENT
MAKES 6

1 (215-g/7½-oz) packet frozen puff
pastry, thawed
1 egg yolk
Filling
100 g/4 oz button mushrooms, sliced
50 g/2 oz butter or margarine
25 g/1 oz plain flour
300 ml/½ pint milk
150 ml/¼ pint hot chicken stock
225 g/8 oz ham, diced
salt and freshly ground black pepper
chopped parsley to garnish

Set the oven at moderately hot (200 C, 400 F, gas 6). Roll out the pastry to a thickness of about 5 mm/¼ in on a floured surface. Using a 7.5-cm/3-in diameter pastry cutter, cut out 12 rounds. Then, using a 5-cm/2-in cutter, cut out the centre of six rounds to make six rings and six lids.

Brush round the edges of the large rounds with a little cold water. Place the rings of pastry on top, pressing gently to seal them together.

Dampen a large baking tray. Place the pastry rounds and the lids on it, spacing them well apart. Brush just the top surface of the pastry with a little beaten egg yolk. Bake in the heated oven for about 15 minutes or until risen and golden. Take out, cool slightly, then transfer to a hot serving dish.

To make the filling, fry the mushrooms in half of the butter or margarine for 5 minutes. Set aside.

Heat the remaining fat in a saucepan, stir in the flour and cook gently for 1 minute. Whisk in the milk and stock, bring the mixture to the boil stirring continuously. Reduce the heat and simmer gently for a few minutes, stirring occasionally.

Remove the pan from the heat, stir in the mushrooms and ham. Season with plenty of salt and black pepper. Spoon the filling into the vols-au-vent cases, garnish with chopped parsley and serve at once.

SPINACH TARTLETS

SERVES 4

Pastry
100 g/4 oz plain flour
salt and freshly ground black pepper
50 g/2 oz margarine
1-2 tablespoons cold water
Filling
225 g/8 oz cooked spinach, chopped
¼ teaspoon ground nutmeg
1 egg, beaten
3 tablespoons single cream
75 g/3 oz mature Cheddar cheese, grated
slices of tomato to garnish

Make the shortcrust pastry, following the instructions on page 40. Roll out the dough and use to line four individual fluted flan tins.

Combine the spinach, nutmeg, egg, cream, cheese and plenty of seasoning. Spoon into the uncooked pastry cases. Bake in a moderately hot oven (200 C, 400 F, gas 6) for about 30 minutes, until firm to the touch and the pastry is cooked through. Serve hot, warm or cold. Garnish with sliced tomatoes, cut into quarters.

SAVOURY TARTLETS

MAKES 20-24

Pastry
225 g/8 oz plain flour
pinch of salt
100 g/4 oz margarine
about 3 tablespoons cold water
Filling
350 g/12 oz cream cheese
salt and freshly ground black pepper
2 teaspoons wholegrain mustard
1 teaspoon chopped chives
Toppings
6 slices smoked salmon
6 slices Parma ham
6 rindless rashers lean bacon
6 stuffed green olives
6 canned pineapple chunks, drained
6 black olives
6 whole almonds, shelled

Place the flour and salt in a bowl. Add the margarine and rub in lightly until the mixture resembles fine breadcrumbs. Sprinkle over the water and mix until the mixture combines together to form a dough. Knead together very lightly. Roll out the pastry to a thickness of about 5 mm/¼ in on a floured surface. Using a 7.5-cm/3-in diameter pastry cutter, cut out 20-24 rounds and use to line patty tins. Alternatively, using boat-shaped tins as a guide, cut out pieces of pastry approximately 5-10 mm/¼-½ in larger than the tins and make pastry boats. Prick the lined tins all over and chill for 20 minutes. Set the oven at moderately hot (200 C, 400 F, gas 6). Bake in the heated oven for 8-12 minutes until cooked and lightly browned. Cool on a wire rack.

Lightly beat the cream cheese with a little seasoning, the mustard and chives. Spoon or pipe the filling into the tartlets or boats. Roll the salmon and ham and use to top half of the tartlets. Roll the bacon, place on metal skewers and cook under a hot grill until crisp. Drain and cool on absorbent kitchen paper. Place a stuffed olive, bacon roll and pineapple chunk on each of six cocktail sticks and place one on each of six of the tartlets. Stone the black olives and place an almond in the cavity. Place one of these on each of the remaining tartlets. Serve on a large platter.

Alternatively, all the tartlets may be topped with one topping in which case the quantities of the chosen topping should be increased accordingly.

Spinach Tartlets

ALMOND APPLE SQUARES

MAKES 8

_1 (368-g/13-oz) packet frozen puff pastry,
thawed
2 (225-g/8-oz) packets marzipan
2 large cooking apples, peeled and
cored
milk to glaze
25 g/1 oz flaked almonds to decorate
sifted icing sugar for dusting_

Set the oven to hot (220 C, 425 F, gas 7). Roll the pastry out to a 40-cm/16-in square. Cut into 16 (10-cm/4-in) squares. Divide the marzipan into eight equal pieces and roll each piece into a 7.5-cm/3-in square. Place a piece of marzipan on each pastry square.

Slice each apple into four rings and place a ring on top of the marzipan. Cover with a second square of pastry, dampening with water and sealing the edges well. Brush with milk and sprinkle with flaked almonds. Bake in the heated oven for 20 minutes. Sprinkle with sifted icing sugar. Serve warm or cold with lightly-whipped double cream.

HONEYED WALNUT TART

SERVES 6 - 8

_**Pastry**
175 g/6 oz plain wholemeal flour
50 g/2 oz plain flour
pinch of salt
175 g/6 oz butter
25 g/1 oz light soft brown sugar
1 egg yolk
Filling
2 oranges
1 lemon
225 g/8 oz walnut pieces
175 g/6 oz clear honey
1 tablespoon demerara sugar
150 ml/¼ pint double cream to decorate_

To make the pastry place both of the flours and salt in a bowl. Rub in the butter until the mixture resembles fine breadcrumbs. Add the sugar and egg yolk. Mix to form a dough. Knead lightly and use to line a 23-cm/9-in flan tin. Bake 'blind' (see page 36) in a moderately hot oven (200 C, 400 F, gas 6) for 20 minutes.

Pare the rind from the oranges and lemon and cut into thin strips. Place in a saucepan, cover with water and bring to the boil, then simmer for 15 minutes. Drain and mix with the walnuts, juice of half the lemon and the honey. Spread evenly over the flan case and sprinkle the sugar over the top. Bake in a moderately hot oven (200 C, 400 F, gas 6) for 10-15 minutes. Leave until just warm.

Whip the cream until stiff, spoon into a piping bag fitted with a star-shaped nozzle and pipe around the edge of the flan just before serving.

MINCE PIES

MAKES 20 - 24

_350 g/12 oz plain flour
pinch of salt
175 g/6 oz butter or margarine, chilled
and diced
50 g/2 oz icing sugar, sifted
1 egg yolk
3-4 tablespoons water
450 g/1 lb mincemeat
a little milk_

Put the flour and salt into a mixing bowl. Rub the butter or margarine into the flour until the mixture resembles fine breadcrumbs. Stir in the icing sugar.

Mix the egg yolk with the water and gradually stir it into the mixture to make a soft, but not sticky, dough. Turn out on to a floured surface. Knead gently until smooth, then wrap and chill for 20-30 minutes or until firm.

Roll the pastry out to 3-mm/⅛-in thick and cut out 20-24 circles large enough to line the base of patty tins. Cut out a further 20-24 small circles to cover the pies. Line the patty tins with the larger circles of pastry. Put a small spoonful of mincemeat into each pastry case. Brush the edges of the lids with a little cold water and place them on the pies. Press down firmly to seal the edges. Roll out any pastry trimmings and cut out stars or leaf shapes. Cut a small hole in each pie and decorate with the pastry shapes. Brush with a little milk.

Bake in a moderate oven (180 C, 350 F, gas 4) for 20-25 minutes until golden brown. Sprinkle with icing sugar and allow to cool in the tins for 5 minutes before transferring to a wire rack. Store in an airtight tin.

Party Tip

During the festive season why not throw the simplest party of all, with plenty of warm mince pies and mulled wine. For a real treat, make it a mid-afternoon gathering and allow your guests to linger into the evening or organise a healthy late afternoon walk just before the evening draws in.

Savoury Moulds & Mousses

One of the most important points to remember when you serve food for any special occasion is that it must look good as well as taste good. Turned out or set in attractive dishes, moulds and mousses can look very appetising when garnished.

Here you will find a selection of savoury dishes which could well form part of a buffet meal or make an excellent course in their own right. A light fish mousse served with some new potatoes and buttered vegetables or a salad may be more suitable for the main course than a very rich dish.

Alternatively, the recipes which follow are all ideal for the first course of the meal. Remember to offer crisp toast, hot bread or crunchy biscuits to complement the soft, light mousses and moulds.

AVOCADO MOUSSE
SERVES 6

3 ripe avocados
juice of 1 lemon
2 tablespoons French dressing
25 g/1 oz powdered gelatine
150 ml/¼ pint chicken stock
150 ml/¼ pint dry white wine
150 ml/¼ pint thick mayonnaise
150 ml/¼ pint double or whipping cream, whipped
1 teaspoon horseradish sauce
salt and freshly ground black pepper
sprigs of watercress to garnish

Peel and slice the avocados. Mix with the lemon juice and French dressing and blend in a liquidiser or sieve to make a purée. Meanwhile, dissolve the gelatine in a little of the chicken stock over a pan of hot water. Add the remaining stock and the white wine. Stir the mayonnaise and cream into the avocado purée. Stir in gelatine mixture evenly and add the horseradish sauce, salt and pepper. Turn into an oiled 23-cm/9-in ring mould. Cover with cling film and chill until set.

To serve, turn the mousse out on to a flat serving dish. Garnish with watercress.

ASPIC-COATED EGGS
SERVES 6

6 hard-boiled eggs
15 g/½ oz aspic crystals
600 ml/1 pint water
salt and freshly ground black pepper
25 g/1 oz peas, cooked
2 slices ham, tongue or salami, cut into small strips

Shell the eggs. Make the aspic, following the instructions on the packet. Pour a little of the aspic into the serving dish and leave to cool and set. When set carefully chop the aspic on the plate.

Pour a little of the remaining aspic into six oval moulds or ramekins. Leave until almost set. Carefully arrange the strips of meat and peas in the aspic. Add the eggs to the moulds, pour over a little more aspic and leave to set. Continue in this fashion until all the aspic and peas and meat have been used and the moulds are full.

Chill the eggs until completely set. Carefully dip each mould in hot water for a few seconds to turn out. Arrange the eggs attractively on the serving plate with the chopped aspic. Serve chilled.

INDIVIDUAL SALMON MOUSSES

SERVES 4

25 g/1 oz butter
1 small onion, finely chopped
200 ml/7 fl oz fish stock
7 g/¼ oz powdered gelatine
2-3 tablespoons dry white wine
1 (212-g/7½-oz) can salmon, drained
salt and freshly ground black pepper
pinch of grated nutmeg
150 ml/¼ pint double or whipping cream
Garnish
lemon twists
sprigs of dill

Melt the butter in a frying pan and gently cook the onion until soft but not browned. Add the stock and simmer for about 10 minutes to reduce. Remove from the heat and sprinkle the gelatine over. Stir, then leave until the gelatine has dissolved and the mixture is clear. Add the wine. Meanwhile, pound or liquidise the salmon to make a paste, then beat in the gelatine liquid and add seasoning and nutmeg to taste.

Chill until just beginning to set. Lightly whip the cream and fold into the mixture. Turn into four small moulds (or turn into a fish mould) and chill. Serve chilled garnished with lemon twists and sprigs of fresh dill. Offer some crisp Granary toast or melba toast to accompany the mousse.

Aspic-coated Eggs

Tuna Creams

TUNA CREAMS
S E R V E S 4

150 ml/¼ pint natural yogurt
100 g/4 oz cream cheese
4 tablespoons thick mayonnaise
1 tablespoon lemon juice
salt and freshly ground black pepper
4 spring onions, finely sliced
1 hard-boiled egg, chopped
2 gherkins, chopped
1 (198-g/7-oz) can tuna, drained and
flaked
15 g/½ oz powdered gelatine
2 tablespoons water
Garnish
slices of cucumber
slices of lemon

Combine the yogurt, cream cheese, mayonnaise and lemon juice, and season well.

Mix together the spring onion, hard-boiled egg, gherkins and tuna, and fold into the yogurt mixture. Blend the mixture in a liquidiser or food processor until smooth. Dissolve the gelatine in the water in a basin over a pan of hot water. Stir into the yogurt mixture.

Spoon into four individual dishes and chill until set. Serve garnished with a twist of cucumber and a slice of lemon. Offer warmed bread with the mousse. If you have the time make some attractive rolls (see page 69).

SMOKED FISH MOUSSE
S E R V E S 4 - 6

350 g/12 oz smoked cod, haddock or coley
150 ml/¼ pint milk
25 g/1 oz butter
2 tablespoons flour
salt and freshly ground black pepper
2 eggs, separated
15 g/½ oz powdered gelatine
1 tablespoon water
150 ml/¼ pint soured cream
2 tablespoons chopped chives
grated rind of 1 lemon
Garnish
sprigs of watercress
lemon twists

Cook the fish in the milk for 10-15 minutes until firm. Drain, reserving 150 ml/¼ pint cooking liquor, made up with more milk if necessary. Cool the fish, remove all skin and bones, and flake the flesh.

Melt the butter in a pan, stir in the flour and cook for 1 minute, then gradually add the reserved milk. Bring to the boil for 1 minute, then add salt and pepper to taste. Remove from the heat and beat in the egg yolks, one at a time. Blend the sauce with the fish in a liquidiser or food processor until smooth.

Dissolve the gelatine in the water in a basin over a pan of hot water. Stir into the sauce, then add the soured cream, chives and lemon rind. Whisk the egg whites until stiff and fold into the mixture. Pour into six individual moulds (about 150-ml/¼-pint capacity) and chill until set.

To serve dip the moulds into hot water for a few seconds and turn the mousses out on to six small plates.

Garnish each mousse with a small sprig of watercress and a twist of lemon.

Party Tip
Make the mousse in a large ring mould and fill the middle with watercress. Garnish with lemon twists and serve as the centrepiece for a buffet lunch.

EGG AND BLUE CHEESE MOUSSE

SERVES 4 - 6

100 g/4 oz blue cheese, mashed
½ cucumber, peeled, grated and drained
3 tablespoons chopped parsley
½ canned pimiento, drained and chopped
½ onion, finely chopped
15 g/½ oz powdered gelatine
150 ml/¼ pint water
3 tablespoons lemon juice
300 ml/½ pint double cream, lightly whipped
salt and freshly ground black pepper
6 hard-boiled eggs, sliced
150 ml/¼ pint aspic jelly

Mix together the cheese, cucumber, parsley, pimiento and onion. Dissolve the gelatine with the water in a bowl over a saucepan of simmering water, add lemon juice and add to the cheese mixture. Fold in the cream and season. When the mixture is on the point of setting, spoon a layer of the mixture into a glass dish. Cover with a layer of egg slices and repeat the layers until the dish is three-quarters full, ending with a layer of mousse. Make a circle of egg round the edge. Chill. Meanwhile, make up the aspic jelly and cool before spooning over the mousse. Allow to set. Serve chilled with a fresh green salad.

CREAMY CHICKEN MOUSSE

SERVES 6 - 8

150 ml/¼ pint chicken aspic
½ cucumber
1 large red pepper, deseeded and chopped
15 g/½ oz gelatine
300 ml/½ pint hot water
50 g/2 oz butter
25 g/1 oz plain flour
1 chicken stock cube
300 ml/½ pint milk
2 eggs, separated
salt and pepper
4 spring onions, trimmed and finely chopped
225 g/8 oz cooked chicken, finely chopped or minced
freshly grated nutmeg

Pour the aspic into the base of a lightly oiled 1.15-1.4-litre/2-2½-pint ring tin or mould. Cut a few thin slices off the cucumber and set them in the aspic with a little of the chopped pepper. Chill until set. Dissolve the gelatine in a little of the hot water, in a basin over a saucepan of simmering water.

Melt the butter in a saucepan, then stir in the flour and stock cube. Gradually pour in the remaining water and the milk and bring to the boil stirring continuously. Cook for 2 minutes until smooth and thick. Remove the pan from the heat and immediately beat in the egg yolks. Stir in seasoning to taste, the onions, chicken and a little nutmeg to taste. Lastly stir in the dissolved gelatine. Set aside to cool.

When the mixture has cooled and is beginning to set, whisk the egg whites until they stand in stiff peaks and carefully fold them into the mixture. Turn it into the tin over the layer of aspic and chill thoroughly until set.

To serve, put the mould in a bowl of hot water for a few seconds, then invert it on to a flat platter. Chop the remaining cucumber and mix it with the remaining red pepper. Fill the middle of the mousse with this mixture just before serving.

Vegetables & Salads

In this chapter you will find recipes which are intended as accompaniments to a main course, a few of which can be served as a first course and others which can be offered with a selection of buffet dishes.

In addition to following a set recipe, try preparing a variety of very simple salads by combining fresh vegetables in season and dressing them with oil and vinegar. Make use of the many types of lettuce which are available either as a base for an elaborate salad or served plain, with just some spring onions and watercress.

Pep up a simple vinaigrette dressing with mustard, honey, garlic, herbs or grated lemon rind. Flavour mayonnaise in the same way and thin it down with a little cream to make a rich dressing. For a light alternative, use natural yogurt instead.

The most important point to remember when preparing vegetable dishes is that the basic ingredients should be the best quality and the freshest available.

POTATO CROQUETTES
SERVES 4

*675 g/1 ½ lb potatoes, peeled and
cooked (see page 16)
about 200 ml/7 fl oz hot milk
salt and freshly ground black pepper
40 g/1 ½ oz butter or margarine
a little grated nutmeg
2 egg yolks
2 tablespoons flour
1 egg, beaten
50 g/2 oz dried breadcrumbs
oil for deep frying*

Drain the potatoes well. Mash them thoroughly or press through a sieve. Beat in the hot milk a little at a time and season to taste with salt and pepper. Add the butter or margarine piece by piece, beating between each addition until a light, fluffy purée is formed.

Beat the egg yolks into the potato purée, then stiffen it by beating in the flour. Shape the mixture into balls about 2.5-cm/1-in in diameter, or into small, cork-shaped rolls. Dip these in beaten egg and coat with dried breadcrumbs. Heat the oil for deep frying to 190 C/375 F. Fry the croquettes in the oil, a few at a time, until crisp and golden. Drain on absorbent kitchen paper. Serve hot.

DUCHESSE POTATOES
MAKES ABOUT 20

*1.25 kg/2 ½ lb potatoes, peeled and
quartered
salt
75 g/3 oz butter or margarine
freshly ground black pepper
1 large egg, lightly beaten
beaten egg for glazing*

Cook the potatoes in boiling salted water until tender – about 15-20 minutes. Drain and mash well.

Set the oven at moderately hot (200 C, 400 F, gas 6). Beat in the butter or margarine, pepper and egg. Mix well, allow to cool and place in a large piping bag fitted with a large star nozzle. Pipe rosettes on to a lightly greased baking tray.

Brush the potato with beaten egg and cook for 15-20 minutes in the centre of the heated oven.

Beetroot and Potato Salad Platter and Curried Potato Salad (both recipes on page 51)

STUFFED CABBAGE LEAVES

MAKES 10-12

10-12 large cabbage leaves
Filling
1 onion, grated
1 (50-g/2-oz) can fillets of anchovies,
chopped
1 (195-g/7-oz) can sweetcorn, drained
225 g/8 oz long-grain rice, cooked
salt and freshly ground black pepper
Garnish
black olives

Cut away the thick stem from each cabbage leaf. Plunge into boiling water and blanch for one minute. Cool in cold water and drain thoroughly. Trim the leaves into neat squares.

Mix together the ingredients for the filling and season with plenty of salt and black pepper. Put a little of this mixture into each piece of cabbage and roll up. Arrange on a serving dish and garnish with black olives.

Stuffed Cabbage Leaves

BUTTERED CARROT STICKS

SERVES 4

1 kg/2¼ lb carrots
salt and freshly ground black pepper
75 g/3 oz butter
chopped parsley to garnish

Scrape the carrots and cut in four lengthways, then cut each quarter in 5-cm/2-in long strips.

Cook the carrots in boiling salted water for 8-10 minutes or until just tender. Drain well.

Melt the butter in a saucepan, add the carrots and cook over a low heat for a few minutes. Season to taste. Transfer to a warmed serving dish, sprinkle with parsley and serve at once.

MIXED VEGETABLE FRITTERS

S E R V E S 6

(Illustrated on page 53)

*1 kg/2¼ lb vegetables in season
(carrots, broccoli, cauliflower,
courgettes, aubergines, mushrooms
or okra)
oil for deep frying*
Batter
*225 g/8 oz plain flour
salt and freshly ground black pepper
250 ml/8 fl oz water
1-2 tablespoons oil
2 egg whites*

Sift the flour, salt and pepper into a bowl, make a well in the centre and add the water and oil. Beat until smooth. Leave the batter to stand for about an hour. Just before using the batter, whisk the egg whites until stiff, but not dry, and fold into the batter.

Prepare all the vegetables by trimming and peeling them, if necessary, and cutting them into small strips and slices or breaking them into florets. Heat the oil in a deep pan to 190C/375F or until it spits when a little of the batter is dropped in.

Dip the prepared vegetables one at a time into the batter, making sure that they are well coated, then drop them into the oil, a few at a time and deep fry until golden and crisp (the length of cooking time will depend on the vegetables used). Drain thoroughly on absorbent kitchen paper and serve hot.

HOT RICE MOULD

S E R V E S 6 - 8

*225 g/8 oz long-grain brown rice
salt and freshly ground black pepper
175 g/6 oz Cheddar cheese, grated
4 tablespoons chopped parsley
50 g/2 oz butter or margarine
1 onion, finely chopped
1 clove garlic, finely chopped
4 celery sticks, finely chopped
225 g/8 oz mushrooms, sliced*

Cook the rice in boiling salted water for about 45 minutes, or until tender. Drain but do not rinse. Immediately fold in the Cheddar cheese, chopped parsley and pepper to taste.

Melt the butter and fry the onion, garlic and celery for about 5 minutes. Add the mushrooms and fry for a few minutes.

Grease a 1.15-litre/2-pint ring mould. Layer the rice and mushroom mixtures in the ring mould, ending with a layer of rice. Press down well. Bake for 15 minutes in a moderate oven (180C, 350F, gas 4).

To turn out, put a flat plate over the top of the mould. Turn over quickly and carefully lift it away.

VEGETABLE MEDLEY

S E R V E S 4 - 6

(Illustrated on page 53)

*1 aubergine
salt and freshly ground black pepper
1 red pepper, deseeded
1 green pepper, deseeded
1 onion
2-3 courgettes
2-3 tablespoons oil
2 cloves garlic, crushed
1 (396-g/14-oz) can chopped tomatoes
1 (225-g/8-oz) can sweetcorn, drained
50 g/2 oz walnut pieces
1 tablespoon chopped parsley to garnish*

Neatly dice the aubergine, sprinkle it with salt and set aside for 30 minutes. Cut the peppers and onion in half and cut into slices. Slice the courgettes. To give the courgettes an attractive flower-like appearance use a canelling knife to cut thin grooves lengthways down the courgette before slicing.

Heat the oil in a pan and fry the peppers, onion and garlic gently for 5 minutes, stirring frequently. Rinse the aubergine and pat dry. Add the aubergine to the pan with the courgettes and cook for a further 10 minutes. Add the tomatoes and sweetcorn and season well with salt and black pepper. Cover the pan and simmer for about 15 minutes or until the vegetables are cooked and the tomato mixture is thick. Stir in the walnut pieces and heat through. Taste and adjust the seasoning if necessary. Serve hot, garnished with chopped parsley.

STUFFED COURGETTES
SERVES 4 - 6

6-8 large fresh courgettes
salt and freshly ground black pepper
50 g/2 oz rindless bacon, finely chopped
2 cloves garlic, crushed
1 large onion, chopped
2 tablespoons oil
225 g/8 oz tomatoes, peeled and
chopped
50 g/2 oz lentils
1 tablespoon chopped parsley
50 g/2 oz grated Cheddar cheese

Wash and dry the courgettes, halve lengthways, scoop out the centre flesh, and chop. Cook the courgette shells in boiling salted water for 5 minutes. Drain. Sauté the bacon, garlic and onion in the oil. Stir in the tomatoes, courgette flesh, lentils and enough water to cover. Simmer for about 20 minutes or until the lentils are tender and the water has been absorbed. Sprinkle over the chopped parsley and cheese. Arrange the stuffed courgettes side by side in a greased ovenproof dish. Grill the courgettes for 5-10 minutes or until golden. Serve hot or cold.

Stuffed Courgettes

CHICKEN AND ORANGE SALAD
SERVES 4

450 g/1 lb cooked chicken
50 g/2 oz cream cheese
2 teaspoons horseradish sauce
150 ml/¼ pint single cream
1 tablespoon chopped parsley
salt and freshly ground black pepper
2 oranges

Cut the chicken into bite-sized cubes. Mash the cheese with a fork and beat to a smooth sauce with the horseradish and the cream. Stir in the chopped parsley and seasoning. Halve the oranges and vandyke (see page 17). Scoop out the orange flesh, discarding the pips and membranes, and cut into small pieces; mix with the chicken. Stir the cream sauce into the chicken and orange mixture.

Pile the mixture into the orange shells and serve thoroughly chilled.

BEETROOT AND POTATO SALAD PLATTER

SERVES 4 - 6

3 potatoes, scrubbed
salt and freshly ground black pepper
3 celery sticks
1 large beetroot, cooked and peeled
150 ml/¼ pint mayonnaise
lemon juice
lettuce leaves (optional)
1 tablespoon chopped chives
To serve
selection of cold meats

Cook the potatoes in their skins, in boiling salted water, for about 20 minutes, or until just tender. Drain and allow to cool. Peel the potatoes and cut them into 1-cm/½-in dice. Cut the celery and beetroot into similar sized dice. Mix the potato, celery and beetroot cubes and fold in the mayonnaise. Season to taste with salt, pepper and a little lemon juice. Spoon the mixture into a serving bowl lined with lettuce leaves, if liked, and sprinkle with the chives.

To make meat cones, make a cut from the centre of each slice of meat and roll up to form cones. Use to surround the salad.

POTATO CURRIED SALAD

SERVES 4

6 large potatoes, peeled and cut
into 1-cm/½-in dice
salt and freshly ground black pepper
1 teaspoon concentrated curry paste
1 teaspoon curry powder
2 teaspoons mango or other chutney
1 (150-ml/¼ pint) carton natural yogurt
1 hard-boiled egg
Garnish
½ cucumber
small bunch of watercress or a few
chopped chives

Cook the potatoes in boiling salted water for 5 minutes, or until just tender. Drain and cool. Mix the curry paste and chutney into the yogurt and add salt and pepper to

taste. Stir in the diced potatoes. Halve the egg and separate the white from the yolk. Press the white and yolk, separately, through a sieve. Arrange the potato mixture in a bowl and sprinkle or spoon the sieved egg white and yolk on top to make an attractive pattern. Using a canelling knife, cut thin grooves down the length of the cucumber, then slice the cucumber. Cut the cucumber slices in half and arrange them round the edge of the bowl. Garnish with a few sprigs of watercress or a few chopped chives.

STUFFED ARTICHOKES

SERVES 4

4 globe artichokes
salt and freshly ground black pepper
2 tablespoons wine vinegar
½ teaspoon made mustard
4 tablespoons double cream
2 tablespoons mayonnaise
100 g/4 oz ham, cut into strips
2 hard-boiled eggs, quartered
100 g/4 oz canned mussels, drained and
halved
2 tomatoes, peeled and chopped

Remove the stalks and cook the artichokes in boiling salted water for 50 minutes. Take the artichokes out of the water, drain, and pull out the inner leaves and the choke so that the firm base of the artichoke can be seen.

Mix the wine vinegar with the mustard and seasoning to taste; pour into the artichokes and leave for 30 minutes. Whip the cream lightly and mix with the mayonnaise. Pour in the vinegar mixture from the artichokes and add the ham strips. Fill the artichokes with the eggs, mussels and tomatoes. Spoon over the mayonnaise mixture.

GUACAMOLE SALAD

SERVES 4 OR 6 AS A STARTER

450 g/1 lb new potatoes, scrubbed
salt and freshly ground black pepper
2 ripe avocados
1 small onion, grated
1 small green pepper, deseeded and
finely diced
1 tablespoon lemon juice
few drops of Tabasco sauce

Cook the potatoes in boiling salted water for 15 minutes, or until tender. Drain the potatoes, dice and cool them.

Peel and mash the avocados and stir in the onion, green pepper, lemon juice and the cooled potatoes. Season to taste with salt, pepper and a few drops of Tabasco. Chill until needed, then serve in the centre of a green salad.

RICE SALAD

SERVES 6 - 8

225 g/8 oz long-grain rice
600 ml/1 pint chicken stock or
vegetable stock
1 large red pepper, deseeded and chopped
1 large green pepper, deseeded and
chopped
1 bunch spring onions, trimmed and
chopped
175 g/6 oz hazelnuts or walnuts, chopped
4 sticks celery, chopped
25 g/1 oz raisins
4 tablespoons olive oil
6 tomatoes, peeled and chopped
½ cucumber, lightly peeled and chopped
2 dessert apples, cored and chopped
juice of ½ lemon
150 ml/¼ pint mayonnaise
salt and pepper

Put the rice in a saucepan and pour in the stock. Bring to the boil, then reduce the heat and cover the pan. Simmer gently for 20-25 minutes or until all the liquid has been absorbed.

Stir the peppers, onions, nuts, celery, raisins and oil into the hot rice, cover and set aside to cool. When the rice is cold, add the tomatoes, cucumber and apple and stir in the lemon juice. Add the mayonnaise and mix well. Taste and add seasoning, then chill lightly before serving.

TURNED-OUT SALAD

SERVES 4

300 ml/½ pint water
pinch of salt
bunch of fresh mixed herbs
(for example parsley, sage, dill, chervil,
tarragon, thyme)
1 small cauliflower, broken into florets
225 g/8 oz frozen peas
25 g/1 oz powdered gelatine
450 ml/¾ pint white wine
salt and freshly ground black pepper
pinch of sugar
few drops of lemon juice
2 hard-boiled eggs, sliced
1 red pepper, deseeded and cut
into strips
few sprigs of mint

Bring the water and salt to the boil in a pan. Place the mixed herbs in the boiling water, cover the pan and simmer over a low heat for 10 minutes. Strain. Place the cauliflower florets in the herb stock, cover and simmer over a low heat for 15 minutes. Take the florets out of the pan, plunge into cold water, drain and cool.

Place the peas in the stock, cover and cook over a low heat for about 3 minutes. Remove from the pan, plunge into cold water, drain and leave to cool. Take the pan off the heat, sprinkle with the gelatine and stir until thoroughly dissolved. Add enough white wine to make the stock up to 750 ml/1 ¼ pints, topping up with water if necessary. Season with the salt, pepper, sugar and lemon juice and leave to cool.

Rinse out a 1.4-litre/2½-pint jelly mould with cold water and pour 'aspic' into it up to 5-mm/¼-in high. Place in the refrigerator to set. Arrange the slices of egg and strips of pepper on top of the mould. Pour over a little more 'aspic' and return to the refrigerator to set, then add half the peas followed by all the cauliflower. Cover with more 'aspic' and return to the refrigerator to set. Top with the remaining peas and pour on the remaining gelatine liquid. Return to the refrigerator for 3-4 hours to set completely. Before serving, loosen the edges with a sharp knife. Dip the mould in hot water for a few seconds and turn out the salad mould on to a plate. Garnish with mint sprigs or any of the fresh herbs used in the herb stock.

Mixed Vegetable Fritters and Vegetable Medley (both recipes on page 49)

Hot Puddings

Sometimes, particularly in winter, it is nice to keep the main course simple and light, then serve a hot, heart-warming pudding to follow. Remember to make plenty of traditional, creamy custard sauce or serve whipped cream with the pudding. Surprisingly, good vanilla ice cream can make a wonderful, contrasting accompaniment for a variety of hot puddings.

The most obvious occasion on which to abandon the main course completely is Shrove Tuesday – pancake day. Serve a very simple meal or just make a pile of delicious pancakes and have plenty of lemon juice and caster sugar with them.

An afternoon tea gathering offers the opportunity for a great deal of waffle! Make sure your guests have not partaken of a heavy lunch, then serve lots of hot, crisp waffles with as many different toppings as you can prepare. What a treat!

CRÊPES SUZETTE

SERVES 4

Pancake batter
100 g/4 oz plain flour
2 eggs
300 ml/½ pint milk
2 tablespoons water
butter or oil for cooking

To serve
grated rind and juice of 1 orange
50 g/2 oz butter
3 tablespoons caster sugar
4 tablespoons brandy
2 tablespoons orange-flavoured liqueur

To make the batter, sift the flour into a bowl and make a well in the middle. Add the eggs and a little of the milk. Beat the eggs with the milk, gradually working in the flour and pouring in the remaining milk, to make a smooth batter. Beat in the water, then set aside for at least 30 minutes.

Heat a little butter or oil in a frying pan and pour in enough batter to cover the base of the pan, tilting the pan to give a thin even coating. Cook until golden underneath then turn the pancake over and cook the second side. Cook all the pancakes in the same way, stacking them and sprinkling each one with a little caster sugar to prevent them sticking together. Keep hot until all are cooked.

To serve the pancakes, put the orange rind and juice in a large frying pan or chaffing pan at the table. Add the butter and sugar and heat until the butter melts and the sugar has dissolved. Fold the pancakes into quarters and arrange them in the pan, turning each one in the juices. Heat for a few minutes, then pour in the brandy and liqueur. Set light to the alcohol and serve the pancakes as soon as the flames have died down.

Crêpes Suzette

WAFFLES

MAKES ABOUT 10

75 g/3 oz self-raising flour
50 g/2 oz butter
1 egg
300 ml/½ pint milk
pinch of salt

Sift the flour into a bowl and rub in the butter until the mixture resembles fine breadcrumbs. Make a well in the centre. Whisk the egg and milk together and gradually beat into the flour mixture to give a smooth batter.

To cook the waffles use the waffle plates of a contact grill or a heated waffle iron. Pour enough batter in to cover the plates and cook for 3 minutes until golden. Serve with any of the following toppings or with butter.

Orange cinnamon syrup Mix together 6 table-spoons golden syrup with the grated rind of 1 orange and ½ teaspoon ground cinnamon. Pour over the warm or cooled waffles.

Strawberry cream Whip 150 ml/¼ pint double cream with 2 tablespoons icing sugar until stiff. Fold in 225 g/8 oz hulled and halved strawberries. Serve with cooled waffles for a refreshing summer treat.

Waffles

Bananas and Brown Sugar Slice 4 bananas and sprinkle with 4 tablespoons lemon juice to prevent discoloration. Add 2 tablespoons soft brown sugar and 150 ml/¼ pint double cream. Pour over the waffles to serve.

Apple and Honey Mix 2 peeled, cored and sliced dessert apples with 1 tablespoon lemon juice and 4 tablespoons honey. Serve with warm or cold waffles.

To make butter shapes Chill the butter until hard, slice into 5-mm/¼-in slices and use shaped cutters to stamp out attractive shapes such as stars, moons or fluted circles.

HAZELNUT PANCAKES
S E R V E S 2 - 4

100 g/4 oz plain flour
pinch of salt
1 egg
300 ml/½ pint milk
2 tablespoons oil
175 g/6 oz ground hazelnuts
300 ml/½ pint double cream
75 g/3 oz icing sugar

Sieve the flour and salt into a bowl. Make a well in the centre and add the egg and half the milk. Beat until smooth, then gradually beat in the remaining milk and 1 teaspoon of the oil. Set aside. Whip half the cream with half the icing sugar until thick. Fold in half the hazelnuts.

Heat a little of the remaining oil in a 25-cm/10-in pancake pan. Spoon in a quarter of the batter and tip to cover the pan. Cook for 1 minute, then turn over and cook for about 30 seconds. Slide the pancake out of the pan and keep hot while you cook the remaining three pancakes in the same way.

Spread the pancakes with the hazelnut filling and roll up. Arrange on a warmed serving dish. Gently heat the remaining hazelnuts, cream and icing sugar in a saucepan, and pour over the pancakes.

QUEEN OF PUDDINGS
S E R V E S 6

300 ml/½ pint milk
100 g/4 oz caster sugar
3 eggs, separated
75 g/3 oz soft white breadcrumbs
3 tablespoons strawberry jam
1 tablespoon lemon juice
fresh or glacé cherries and toasted
flaked almonds to decorate

Grease a medium-sized pie dish. Whisk the milk, 25 g/1 oz of the caster sugar and the egg yolks together. Pour over the breadcrumbs in a mixing bowl and leave to soak for 15 minutes. Mix the jam and lemon juice together. Put the softened crumbs and milk mixture into the pie dish and bake in a moderate oven (180 C, 350 F, gas 4) for 20 minutes. Remove from the oven and spread with the jam mixture.

Whisk the egg whites until they stand in stiff peaks, then gradually whisk in the remaining sugar, 1 table-spoon at time, until the meringue is stiff and glossy. Fit a

piping bag with a large star-shaped nozzle and pipe rosettes of meringue over the pudding. Dust with a little extra caster sugar, if liked, and bake for a further 15 minutes or until the meringue is set and golden. Decorate with fresh or glacé cherries and toasted flaked almonds.

FRUIT TART
S E R V E S 6

350 g/12 oz plain flour
pinch of salt
175 g/6 oz margarine
about 4 tablespoons water
grated rind of 1 large orange
Filling
2 tablespoons rum (optional)
100 g/4 oz no-need-to-soak dried apricots,
roughly chopped
450 g/1 lb cooking apples, peeled,
cored and sliced
50 g/2 oz caster sugar
beaten egg or milk to glaze

If using the rum, warm it and pour over the apricots 2 hours in advance. The apricots may be used unsoaked.

Make the pastry according to the instructions on page 40, adding the orange rind after rubbing in the dry ingredients. Use two-thirds of the pastry to line a 25-cm/10-in flan dish. Layer the apples, sugar and apricots in the flan dish.

Roll out the remaining pastry and cut into 1-cm/½-in strips. Arrange the strips to form a lattice pattern on top of the filling. (Alternatively roll out the remaining pastry just larger than the plate and use a lattice pie cutter to make a decorative lid.)

Brush the pastry with a little beaten egg or milk and bake in a moderately hot oven (200 C, 400 F, gas 6) for 40-45 minutes or until golden brown.

CASTLE PUDDINGS WITH CHOCOLATE SAUCE

MAKES ABOUT 15

100 g/4 oz self-raising flour
1 tablespoon cocoa powder
2 eggs
100 g/4 oz soft margarine
100 g/4 oz caster sugar
Sauce
100 g/4 oz plain chocolate
25 g/1 oz butter
1 tablespoon rum
25 g/1 oz caster sugar (optional)
2-3 tablespoons water

Sieve the flour and cocoa into a bowl. Add the eggs, margarine and sugar. Beat the ingredients well together until they are completely blended. Drop spoonfuls of the mixture into greased dariole moulds so that they are just over half full. Depending on the size, there will be between 12 and 15. Cover each one with a small piece of foil. Put them into a steamer placed over a pan of hot water and cook for about 30 minutes. The water should bubble gently and must not be allowed to run dry.

To make the sauce, break the chocolate into a saucepan. Stir in the butter, rum, sugar (if using) and water. Heat gently until the chocolate has melted, then, stirring continuously, bring the sauce to the boil and simmer for one minute. Pour the chocolate sauce over the top of the puddings and serve at once.

LITTLE ORANGE SOUFFLÉS

SERVES 4

4 large oranges
4 eggs, separated
50 g/2 oz caster sugar
1 tablespoon Cointreau, Grand Marnier
or concentrated orange juice
1 tablespoon icing sugar, sifted

Set the oven at hot (230 C, 450 F, gas 8). Carefully slice the tops from the oranges and scoop out the flesh. Reserve the shells and cut the top edge into a zig-zag pattern. Remove the rind from the caps of the oranges and cut into very thin julienne strips. Cook the orange strips in a little boiling water for 5 minutes to soften. Drain and cool. Extract the juice from the orange flesh and place the juice in a saucepan. Bring to the boil and reduce until just 1 tablespoon orange juice remains.

Place the egg yolks and sugar in a bowl and whisk until very thick and creamy. Add the orange rind, warm orange juice and Cointreau, Grand Marnier or concentrated orange juice. In another bowl, whisk the egg whites until they stand in firm peaks. Fold into the orange mixture using a metal spoon. Spoon equal quantities of the soufflé mixture into each orange case. Place on a baking tray and bake in the heated oven for 10 minutes. While the oranges are still in the oven, sprinkle the tops with the icing sugar. Bake for a further 2-3 minutes, then serve at once.

UPSIDE-DOWN PUDDING

SERVES 6

fresh or canned fruit (for example, pineapple rings, cherries, bananas, pears or plums)
100 g/4 oz butter or margarine
100 g/4 oz caster sugar
2 eggs
100 g/4 oz self-raising flour

Liberally grease a 23-cm/9-in deep cake tin or straight-sided baking dish with butter or margarine and arrange the chosen fruit in the base, in a decorative pattern.

Cream the butter or margarine with the sugar until light and fluffy. Gradually beat in the eggs and fold in the flour. Spoon the mixture over the fruit and bake in a moderate oven (180C, 350F, gas 4) for about 1 hour. Turn the pudding out on to a serving plate or dish. Serve with whipped cream or custard.

Upside-down Pudding

SYRUP TART

SERVES 4 - 6

Pastry
225 g/8 oz plain flour
pinch of salt
100 g/4 oz margarine
about 3 tablespoons cold water
Filling
100 g/4 oz golden syrup
100 g/4 oz fresh white breadcrumbs
grated rind and juice of 1 lemon
grated rind of 1 orange

Set the oven at moderately hot (180, 350F, gas 4). Make the pastry, following the instructions on page 40. Roll out the pastry on a lightly-floured surface and use to line a 23-cm/9-in flan dish. Trim the edges with a sharp knife. Prick the base with a fork and fill with baking beans or line with foil. Bake 'blind' in the heated oven for 10-15 minutes. Heat the syrup and mix in the remaining ingredients. Pour into the pie shell and decorate with the pastry trimmings in a lattice pattern. Reduce the heat to moderate (180C, 350F, gas 4) and bake for 15-20 minutes.

Cool Desserts

Some people look forward to the dessert course more than any other part of the meal. In this chapter you will find dessert recipes which are suitable for all occasions.

Creamy Cheesecake and Orange Roulade are both desserts which can be made in quantities to serve large gatherings. Mocha Charlotte, Raspberry Meringue Nests and Luxurious Stuffed Water Melon all come into the same category. On the other hand, Banana Splits with Fudge sauce are best saved for serving to smaller dinner parties.

If you have problems in deciding just what to serve for dessert then prepare two or three alternative recipes. If you have time, make some crisp home-made biscuits too.

CREAMY CHEESECAKE
SERVES 6 - 8

100 g/4 oz butter, melted
225 g/8 oz digestive biscuits, crushed
1 teaspoon ground cinnamon
450 g/1 lb cream cheese
50 g/2 oz caster sugar
6 tablespoons single cream
15 g/½ oz powdered gelatine
2 tablespoons hot water
300 ml/½ pint double cream
1 egg white, stiffly whisked
Decoration
150 ml/¼ pint whipped cream
fresh soft fruit such as strawberries

Lightly grease a 23-cm/9-in loose-bottomed cake tin. Combine the crushed biscuits, the melted butter and the cinnamon with a wooden spoon. Line the base of the tin with this mixture, pressing it in firmly.

Beat the cream cheese and sugar together with a wooden spoon until smooth and creamy. Dissolve the gelatine in the water. Stir the single cream and dissolved gelatine into the cream cheese mixture. Whip the double cream until it stands in soft peaks and fold into the cheese mixture with the egg white. Spoon the mixture over the biscuit crust. Place in the refrigerator to chill for about 1 hour, or until set.

Decorate with whipped cream and fruit and serve.

CHOCOLATE AND ORANGE MOUSSE
SERVES 6

350 g/12 oz plain chocolate
15 g/½ oz unsalted butter
grated rind of 1 orange
1 tablespoon Cointreau
4 eggs, separated
Decoration
chocolate curls (optional)

Break the chocolate into squares and place in a basin. Stand the basin over a saucepan of simmering water and leave until the chocolate has melted, stirring occasionally.

Remove the basin from the heat and stir in the butter, orange rind and Cointreau. Mix in the egg yolks. Whisk the whites until stiff, then fold into the chocolate mixture.

Spoon into individual serving dishes or cocktail glasses and chill in the refrigerator for at least 1 hour. Decorate with chocolate curls, if used, and serve with crisp dessert biscuits.

Creamy Cheesecake and Chocolate and Orange Mousse

CHOCOLATE AND ORANGE ROULADE
SERVES 6

5 eggs, separated
175 g/6 oz caster sugar
175 g/6 oz plain chocolate, melted
to a cream with 2 tablespoons water
6 large oranges
icing sugar to dust
450 ml/¾ pint double cream

Set the oven at moderate (180C, 350F, gas 4). Whisk the egg whites until stiff. In a separate bowl, whisk the egg yolks and 150 g/5 oz of the sugar until thick and very pale in colour. Add the melted chocolate, then fold in the whisked egg whites. Spread evenly in a Swiss roll tin lined with non-stick paper. Bake in the heated oven for 20-25 minutes until cooked. Cover with a layer of wet kitchen paper. Wrap in cling film and leave overnight. Carefully turn out on to greaseproof paper well dusted with icing sugar and peel off non-stick paper.

For the filling, finely grate the rind of 1 orange. Cut away peel and pith from all the oranges with a sharp knife and remove the segments over a bowl to catch the juice. Whip 300 ml/½ pint of the cream with the orange rind and any juice until thick. Add the remaining sugar to taste. Spread the cream over the sponge. Keep some orange segments for decoration and scatter the rest along the middle of the sponge. Roll up and turn on to a flat serving dish. Dust with icing sugar. Whip the remaining cream until thick and pipe swirls of cream on top, decorate with orange segments and chill.

MOCHA CHARLOTTE
SERVES 6

225 g/8 oz plain chocolate, coarsely
grated
450 ml/¾ pint hot strong coffee
3 eggs, separated
50 g/2 oz caster sugar
15 g/½ oz powdered gelatine
300 ml/½ pint double or whipping cream
Decoration
300 ml/½ pint double cream
langue de chat biscuits
grated chocolate

Dissolve the chocolate in the coffee. Whisk the egg yolks and sugar until thick and pale in colour. Add the chocolate mixture. Return to the rinsed pan and thicken over a gentle heat, without boiling, stirring continuously. Soak the gelatine in 3 tablespoons water and add the soaked gelatine to the chocolate mixture and stir until dissolved. Strain into a bowl and cool. Lightly whip the cream and add to the chocolate mixture. Whisk the egg whites until stiff and fold into the mixture. When on the point of setting, pour into a lightly-oiled straight-sided 18-cm/7-in mould or cake tin with a removable base. Leave in the refrigerator to set.

To serve, turn out and spread a thin layer of whipped cream round the sides. Press the biscuits around. Put the remaining cream into a piping bag and pipe small stars down each biscuit join. Decorate the top with rosettes of cream and grated chocolate.

RUM BABAS

MAKES 16

25 g/1 oz fresh yeast
6 tablespoons warm milk
225 g/8 oz strong white flour
½ teaspoon salt
25 g/1 oz caster sugar
4 eggs, beaten
100 g/4 oz butter, softened
4 tablespoons clear honey
2 tablespoons dark rum
300 ml/½ pint double cream
glacé cherries to decorate

Lightly grease 16 small ring moulds. Cream the yeast with milk and mix in 50 g/2 oz of the flour. Leave in a warm place until frothy, about 20 minutes.

Place the yeast mixture in a bowl and beat in the remaining flour, salt, sugar, eggs and butter. Beat for about 3-4 minutes.

Half-fill the moulds with the batter, cover with cling film and leave in a warm place until the batter rises to fill two-thirds of the moulds.

Set the oven at moderately hot (200 C, 400 F, gas 6).

Bake in the heated oven for 12-15 minutes. Turn out and cool on a wire rack.

Prepare the baba syrup by treating the honey with 4 tablespoons water and the rum. Stir over a low heat until well mixed. Spoon the syrup over the still-hot babas. Leave to cool.

To serve, whip the cream until it stands in soft peaks and pipe the cream into the centres of the babas. Decorate with glacé cherries before serving.

Rum Babas

RASPBERRY MERINGUE NESTS

SERVES 4 - 6

Meringues
4 egg whites
250 g/9 oz icing sugar, sifted
1 teaspoon vanilla essence
Filling
1 small pineapple, peeled, cored and
cut into chunks
3 tablespoons Kirsch (optional)
350 g/12 oz fresh raspberries, hulled
2-3 tablespoons icing sugar, sifted
(optional)
600 ml/1 pint ice cream, flavour
according to taste

Line a baking tray with rice paper or greased grease-proof paper. Mark four (7.5-cm/3-in) circles for four small nests. Place the egg whites in a bowl and place the bowl over a saucepan of simmering water. Gradually add the icing sugar, whisking constantly until the meringue stands in firm peaks. Add the vanilla essence and mix well. Fill a piping bag fitted with a star-shaped nozzle with the meringue mixture. Using the circles as a guideline, pipe continuous circles of meringue, working from the outside to the centre of each nest. Place in a very cool oven (110C, 225F, gas ¼) and bake for 4-5 hours or leave overnight. Cool and remove any paper.

Meanwhile, soak the pineapple chunks in the Kirsch, if used. Purée 225 g/8 oz of the raspberries in a blender. Press through a fine sieve to remove any pips and sweeten, if liked, with icing sugar.

To serve the meringue nests, fill the centres with the ice cream. Add the remaining raspberries and pineapple and top with the raspberry purée.

LUXURIOUS STUFFED WATER MELON

SERVES 4

1 small water melon
3 oranges
juice of ½ lemon
50 g/2 oz sugar
1 tablespoon white rum
1 tablespoon clear honey
4 scoops vanilla ice cream to serve

Slice one-third off the water melon and scoop the flesh out of the slice. Scoop the flesh out of the rest of the melon with a tablespoon, discard the seeds and chop the flesh. Peel 2 oranges, removing all the pith, and separate the segments. Remove the membrane from the segments and cut the flesh into pieces. Mix the orange and melon in a bowl. Cut a decorative pattern around the top of the melon shell and fill the melon with the fruit salad.

Squeeze the juice from the remaining orange. Bring the orange and lemon juice and sugar to the boil in a pan, and simmer, stirring continuously, until the sugar has completely dissolved. Leave to cool and beat in the rum and honey. Pour the syrup over the fruit salad and top with scoops of vanilla ice cream.

BANANA SPLITS WITH FUDGE SAUCE

SERVES 4

4 large ripe bananas, peeled
600 ml/1 pint vanilla ice cream
150 ml/¼ pint double cream
25 g/1 oz walnuts, finely chopped
fresh cherries to decorate (optional)
Sauce
25 g/1 oz plain chocolate
15 g/½ oz butter
2 tablespoons warm milk
100 g/4 oz soft brown sugar
3 teaspoons golden syrup
2-3 drops vanilla essence

First prepare the sauce by melting the chocolate in a bowl over a saucepan of simmering water. Add the butter and stir until smooth and glossy. Gradually blend in the milk. Place this mixture with the sugar and golden syrup in a saucepan and heat gently to dissolve the sugar. Bring to the boil and cook for 5 minutes. Add the vanilla essence and leave to cool.

Meanwhile, split each banana in half and quickly sandwich together with the ice cream in four individual dishes. Whip the cream until it stands in soft peaks. Spoon or pipe decoratively over the bananas and ice cream. Sprinkle with the nuts and decorate with the cherries, if used. Serve with the fudge sauce.

Banana Splits with Fudge Sauce

Baking

Afternoon teas or family gatherings are a good time to serve lots of home-baked goodies. As well as a couple of creamy cakes, there are some attractive small cakes, gingerbread, biscuits and breads included in this chapter.

On Good Friday – or beforehand if you have a freezer – why not turn your hand to making Hot Cross Buns? For dinner parties, lunch or brunch, picnics or parties then home-made bread is always a welcome addition to any menu. Make a splendid array of different rolls, loaves or even French Brioche from this chapter.

When you have the time or feel inspired to do some baking, then remember that breads freeze perfectly, ready for defrosting and warming for any number of occasions.

BASIC WHITE BREAD
MAKES 1 LARGE LOAF OR 2 SMALL LOAVES

450 g/1 lb strong plain flour
1 teaspoon salt
25 g/1 oz butter or margarine
1 tablespoon caster sugar
3 teaspoons dried yeast
300 ml/½ pint lukewarm water

Sift the flour and salt into a bowl, them rub in the butter. Stir in the sugar. Sprinkle the yeast over the water and set aside in a warm place until the yeast has dissolved and the liquid is frothy. Stir to mix.

Make a well in the flour, pour in the yeast liquid and mix with the flour to make a smooth, stiff dough. Turn the dough out on to a floured surface and knead thoroughly for about 10 minutes, or until smooth and elastic. Put in an oiled bowl, cover with oiled cling film and set aside in a warm place until doubled in size. Turn out, knead lightly and divide the dough in half or leave as one loaf.

Grease two 450-g/1-lb loaf tins or one 1-kg/2-lb tin. Put the dough in the tins. Cover with oiled cling film and leave in a warm place until doubled in size.

Bake the loaves in a hot oven (230 C, 450 F, gas 8) for about 40 minutes, or until well risen and browned on top. To test if the bread is cooked, turn it out and tap the base – when cooked through it will sound hollow. Cool on a wire rack.

Making Bread

WHOLEMEAL BREAD
MAKES 1 LARGE LOAF OR 2 SMALL LOAVES

450 g/1 lb wholemeal flour
1 teaspoon salt
25 g/1 oz butter or margarine
1 tablespoon dark soft brown sugar
3 teaspoons dried yeast
300 ml/½ pint lukewarm water
1 tablespoon cracked wheat

Put the flour in a bowl with the salt and rub in the butter or margarine. Stir in the sugar. Sprinkle the yeast over the water, then leave in a warm place until frothy. Stir well. Make a well in the middle of the dry ingredients, pour in the yeast liquid and mix together to make a stiff dough.

Turn the dough out on to a lightly floured surface, and knead thoroughly for about 10 minutes, or until the dough is smooth and elastic. Place in an oiled bowl, cover with oiled cling film and leave in a warm place until doubled in size. Turn out and knead lightly, then divide in half or leave as one loaf.

Grease one 1-kg/2-lb loaf tin or two 450-g/1-lb tins. Place the dough in the tins, cover with cling film and put in a warm place until doubled in size. Brush the top of the loaf or loaves with a little warm water and sprinkle with the cracked wheat. Bake in a hot oven (230 C, 450 F, gas 8) for about 40 minutes or until risen and browned. To test if the loaf is done, turn it out and tap the base. If the bread is cooked it will sound hollow. Cool on a wire rack.

SODA BREAD
MAKES 2 LOAVES

450 g/1 lb plain flour
1 teaspoon bicarbonate of soda
2 teaspoons salt
300 ml/½ pint milk

Sift the flour, bicarbonate of soda and salt into a bowl. Make a well in the middle and pour in the milk. Gradually mix in the dry ingredients to make a smooth, fairly stiff dough. Divide in half and knead lightly until smooth.

Grease a large baking tray. Shape the dough into two round loaves and place them on a tray. Cut a cross in the top of each loaf and bake in a moderately hot oven (190 C, 375 F, gas 5) for 40-45 minutes, or until well risen and golden brown. Cool the loaves on a wire rack, then serve warm with butter.

SHAPING BREAD DOUGH

Bread dough can be shaped in a variety of ways

Bread dough can be shaped into all sorts of attractive loaves or individual rolls. The dough should be allowed to rise for the first time, then knocked backed and shaped before the second rising.

Instead of baking the rolls in tins, to make two round loaves, simply divide the dough in half and shape into smooth rounds. Leave to rise, then cut a cross in the top of each loaf before baking.

To make a cottage loaf, shape two-thirds of the dough into a large round and make a deep depression in the middle. Shape the remaining dough into a small ball and place this in the middle of the round. Leave to rise. Brush with a little beaten egg before baking.

To make a plait, divide the dough into three equal portions and roll them into long strips. Plait them together on the baking tray.

Divide the dough in half and roll each piece into a strip. Twist the two pieces together on a baking tray, arrange the twisted dough into a ring if you like.

Roll the dough into a fairly thick strip, then knot it into figure of eight, tucking the ends underneath on the baking tray.

Shape the dough into a long loaf, French-bread style, and make slits at intervals along it when the dough has risen.

Divide the dough into 12 pieces and shape each into a small round roll. Bake these on a greased baking tray or arrange them fairly close together in a round greased baking tin, so that they join together as they rise and bake to make one loaf. Alternatively, the rolls can be shaped in the same way as the large loaf to make plaits, twists or cottage loaves.

Before they are baked, loaves or rolls can be glazed with beaten egg and sprinkled with seseame or poppy seeds. Cracked wheat can be sprinkled over whole-meal bread.

HOT CROSS BUNS
MAKES 12

450 g/1 lb strong white flour
1 teaspoon caster sugar
25 g/1 oz fresh yeast or 3 teaspoons
dried yeast
150 ml/¼ pint warm milk
75 ml/3 fl oz warm water
1 teaspoon salt
½ teaspoon mixed spice
½ teaspoon ground cinnamon
½ teaspoon grated nutmeg
50 g/2 oz caster sugar
50 g/2 oz butter, softened
1 egg, beaten
100 g/4 oz currants
50 g/2 oz chopped mixed peel
Pastry
50 g/2 oz plain flour
25 g/1 oz margarine
cold water
Glaze
4 tablespoons water and milk, mixed
3 tablespoons caster sugar

Prepare the yeast batter; mix 100 g/4 oz flour, 1 teaspoon sugar, the fresh or dried yeast and the warm milk and water together in a large bowl. Cover and set aside in a warm place until frothy, about 20 minutes.

Mix the remaining flour with the salt, spices and sugar. Add the dry ingredients, softened butter, beaten egg, currants and mixed peel to the yeast batter and mix well to form a soft dough, adding extra flour if the dough is too sticky to handle.

Turn the dough on to a lightly-floured surface and knead until smooth, about 10 minutes by hand or 2-3 minutes with a mixer and dough hook. Shape the dough into a ball and place inside an oiled polythene bag and leave to rise until doubled in size, about 2 hours at room temperature, less in a warm place. Turn out on to a lightly-floured surface, knock-back and knead for 2 minutes.

Divide the dough into 12 equal pieces and shape into buns. Place well apart on greased baking trays. Cover and put to rise for about 30 minutes in a warm place until doubled in size. Set the oven at moderately hot (190 C, 375 F, gas 5). To make the pastry rub the fat into the flour and add cold water to mix to a dough. Roll out thinly and cut into thin strips. Place pastry crosses on each bun.

Bake just above the centre of the heated oven for 15-20 minutes. Remove to a wire rack. Heat the water and milk with the sugar until the sugar has dissolved. Brush over the hot buns twice, leave to cool.

FRENCH BRIOCHE
MAKES 8-10 INDIVIDUAL BRIOCHES

15 g/½ oz fresh yeast or
1½ teaspoons dried yeast
3 tablespoons lukewarm milk
1 tablespoon plus ¼ teaspoon caster sugar
225 g/8 oz strong white flour
¼ teaspoon salt
75 g/3 oz butter or margarine
2 large eggs, well beaten

Set the oven at hot (220 C, 425 F, gas 7). Blend the yeast with the lukewarm milk. Stir in the ¼ teaspoon sugar and 40 g/1½ oz of the flour. Mix well, cover the bowl with a piece of oiled polythene and place aside in a warm place until frothy. Sift the remaining flour with the salt into a bowl, rub in the butter or margarine until the mixture resembles breadcrumbs and then add the 1 tablespoon caster sugar and beaten eggs. Stir in the yeast liquid and mix together to give a fairly stiff dough. Turn out on to a lightly floured surface and knead well. Place the dough in an oiled polythene bag and set aside in a warm place to prove. When the dough has risen, turn it out on to a lightly floured surface, knock-back and knead lightly.

Take three-quarters of the dough and roll it into 8-10 balls. Place each ball in a buttered, fluted brioche tin or deep patty tin. Roll the remaining dough into 8-10 small balls, elongating them slightly to make them pear-shaped. Press a finger into each of the larger balls in the brioche tins to make a well, then fit the stalks of the smaller balls into each one. Place the brioche tins on a baking tray and cover with oiled polythene. Set aside in a warm place until the brioches rise out of the tins, then, if liked, brush them with a little beaten egg. Bake in the centre of the heated oven for about 15 minutes until well risen and brown. Cool on a wire rack.

Hot Cross Buns (opposite)

CRUMPETS
MAKES 12-15

350 g/12 oz strong white flour
1 ½ teaspoons easy-blend dried yeast
350 ml/12 fl oz warm water
½ teaspoon bicarbonate of soda
2 teaspoons salt
150 ml/¼ pint warm milk

Beat the flour, easy-blend yeast and warm water together in a large mixing bowl. Cover with a sheet of oiled polythene and set aside in a warm place until very light and frothy, about 1 hour. Add the bicarbonate of soda and salt to the warm milk and stir into the batter, adding a little extra milk, if necessary, to give a runny batter. Cover again and stand in a warm place until frothy, about 30 minutes to 1 hour.

Heat a griddle or heavy frying pan and very lightly grease the surface. Grease the crumpet rings, or 7.5-cm/3-in plain pastry cutters or poaching rings. Place the rings on the hot griddle or frying pan. Pour about 2 tablespoons of the mixture into each ring. Turn down the heat and cook gently for about 10 minutes or until the crumpets are well set and the bubbles have burst. Remove the rings, turn the crumpets over and cook for a further 2-3 minutes until they are a pale golden brown and thoroughly dried. Repeat until all the mixture has been used up.

GOLDEN COCONUT COOKIES
MAKES 32

2 tablespoons golden syrup
150 g/5 oz butter or margarine
100 g/4 oz caster sugar
75 g/3 oz rolled oats
50 g/2 oz desiccated coconut
150 g/5 oz plain flour, sifted
1 teaspoon bicarbonate of soda
1 tablespoon hot water

Set the oven at moderate (160 C, 325 F, gas 3).

Place the golden syrup in a saucepan with the butter or margarine and sugar. Heat gently until melted and smooth. Allow to cool slightly. Mix the oats with the coconut and flour, then stir into the syrup mixture. Dissolve the bicarbonate of soda in the water and add to the mixture. Combine well.

Divide into 32 balls and place on greased baking trays. Flatten a little with a teaspoon. Bake in the heated oven for 20 minutes or until golden. Allow to cool slightly, then lift off with a palette knife and cool on a wire rack. Store in an airtight tin until required.

GINGER BISCUITS

MAKES 12-14 BISCUITS OR 6-7 GINGERBREAD MEN

225 g/8 oz plain flour
I teaspoon ground ginger
100 g/4 oz butter or margarine
100 g/4 oz muscovado sugar
100 g/4 oz golden syrup
raisins and glacé cherries for
decoration (optional)

Set the oven at moderately hot (190 C, 375 F, gas 5).

Sift the flour with the ginger. Cream the butter or margarine with the sugar until light and fluffy. Add the flour mixture with the syrup and knead until smooth.

Roll out on a lightly floured surface and stamp out rounds with a 7.5-cm/3-in scone or biscuit cutter, or use a gingerbread man or woman cutter and make buttons or eyes, and mouths, from raisins and slivers of glacé cherry. Place on a greased baking tray. Bake in the heated oven for about 20 minutes. Allow to cool on a wire rack.

CHOCOLATE AND ORANGE KISSES

MAKES 14

175 g/6 oz butter or margarine
50 g/2 oz icing sugar, sifted
finely grated rind of I small orange
175 g/6 oz plain flour
25 g/I oz cocoa powder
icing sugar to dust
Butter cream
50 g/2 oz butter
100 g/4 oz icing sugar, sifted
finely grated rind of I orange
I teaspoon orange juice
sifted icing sugar to dust

Set the oven at moderately hot (190 C, 375 F, gas 5).

Prepare the biscuits by creaming the butter or margarine with the icing sugar until light and fluffy. Beat in the orange rind. Sift the flour with the cocoa powder and fold into the creamed mixture, blending well.

Place in a piping bag fitted with a large star-shaped nozzle and pipe 28 small whirls or rosettes on to greased baking trays. Bake in the heated oven for 15 minutes. Remove with a palette knife and cool on a wire rack.

Meanwhile, prepare the butter cream by creaming the butter with the icing sugar until light and fluffy. Add the orange rind and juice, blending well. Use to sandwich the chocolate kisses together. Dust with sifted icing sugar before serving.

Ginger Biscuits

STRAWBERRY CREAM ROLL

S E R V E S   6 - 8

*3 large eggs
75 g/3 oz caster sugar
75 g/3 oz self-raising flour, sifted
4 tablespoons raspberry jam*
Filling
*1-2 tablespoons sherry (optional)
150 ml/¼ pint double cream
2 teaspoons icing sugar
few drops of vanilla essence
2 egg whites
fresh strawberries to decorate*

Set the oven at hot (220 C, 425 F, gas 7). Grease and line a 30 x 23-cm/12 x 9-in Swiss roll tin. Whisk the eggs with the sugar until the mixture is light and creamy and leaves a trail when the whisk is lifted out of the mixture. Fold in the flour, using a metal spoon.

Turn into prepared tin and smooth level with a palette knife. Bake in the heated oven for 7-10 minutes until the sponge begins to shrink from edges of the tin and is pale golden.

Turn out on to a sheet of greaseproof paper dredged with caster sugar. Trim the edges of sponge, spread with warmed jam and roll up tightly. Dredge with caster sugar and cool on a wire tray.

Moisten the jam-filled Swiss roll with the sherry, if liked. Whip the cream until stiff, add the sugar and vanilla. In another bowl, whisk the egg whites until very stiff. Fold the sweetened cream into the stiffly whisked egg whites and spread over the Swiss roll, giving a swirled effect. Decorate with fresh strawberries.

Strawberry Cream Roll

HARLEQUIN COCONUT RING

SERVES 6 - 8

175 g/6 oz butter or margarine
175 g/6 oz caster sugar
3 large eggs, beaten
175 g/6 oz self-raising flour
15 g/½ oz cocoa powder dissolved in
3 tablespoons milk
grated rind of ½ lemon
1 tablespoon lemon juice
yellow food colouring
Topping
225 g/8 oz granulated sugar
4 tablespoons water
1 egg white
50 g/2 oz long-thread coconut, toasted

Set the oven at moderate (180 C, 350 F, gas 4).

Cream the butter or margarine with the sugar until light and fluffy. Add the eggs with a little flour and beat to blend. Fold in the remaining flour. Remove two-thirds of the mixture and mix with the dissolved cocoa blending well. Add the lemon rind, lemon juice and

Harlequin Coconut Ring

colouring to the remaining one-third of the mixture.

Spread the chocolate mixture over the bottom and sides of a greased 1.8-litre/3-pint ring mould. Place the lemon mixture in a piping bag fitted with a large plain nozzle and pipe around the centre of the chocolate mixture. Using a palette knife carefully level the surfaces. Bake in the heated oven for about 40 minutes or until well risen and firm to the touch. Turn out and allow to cool on a wire rack.

To make the topping, dissolve the sugar in the water and boil to 115°C (240°F) or the soft ball stage. To test, drop some of the sugar syrup into a bowl of iced water. The syrup should form a soft ball that will flatten when squeezed between the fingers. Meanwhile, whisk the egg white until it stands in stiff peaks. Pour the sugar syrup on to the egg white and whisk until the topping thickens and turns opaque. Quickly swirl all over the cake and sprinkle with the coconut.

GINGERBREAD

MAKES 1 (20-cm/8-in) SQUARE CAKE

450 g/1 lb plain flour
¼ teaspoon salt
1 tablespoon ground ginger
1 tablespoon ground cinnamon
1 tablespoon ground mixed spice
1 teaspoon ground cloves
225 g/8 oz stoned dates, roughly chopped
100 g/4 oz walnuts, coarsely chopped
225 g/8 oz butter
350 g/12 oz molasses or black treacle
200 g/7 oz dark soft brown sugar
4 large eggs, beaten
1 teaspoon bicarbonate of soda
1 tablespoon warm milk

Set the oven at moderate (180 C, 350 F, gas 4).

Sift the flour, salt and spices into a bowl. Stir in the dates and walnuts. Heat the butter with the molasses or treacle and sugar, stirring until smooth. Add to the flour mixture with the eggs and bicarbonate of soda. Stir in the milk to make a firm but dropping consistency.

Spoon into a greased and lined 20-cm/8-in square cake tin. Bake in the heated oven for 20 minutes, then reduce to cool (150 C, 300 F, gas 2) and bake for 2 hours or until a skewer inserted in the centre comes out clean. Cool on a wire rack.

ICED FANCIES

MAKES ABOUT 30

3 eggs
75 g/3 oz caster sugar
75 g/3 oz self-raising flour
25 g/1 oz butter, melted
Decoration
225 g/8 oz icing sugar
2 tablespoons water
crystallised orange and lemon slices

Set the oven at moderately hot (190 C, 375 F, gas 5). Whisk the eggs and sugar together over a basin of hot water until the mixture leaves a trail from the whisk. Fold in the flour. Fold the butter in gently. Pour the mixture into a well-greased Swiss roll tin, 30 x 22-cm/ 12 x 9-in, and bake in the heated oven for 30 minutes. Turn out and cool on a wire rack.

Sieve the icing sugar into a bowl, and add the water gradually, beating to a coating consistency. Cut the cake into shapes with biscuit cutters; ice and decorate.

Butterfly Cakes and Gingerbread

BUTTERFLY CAKES

MAKES 18

150 g/5 oz butter or margarine
150 g/5 oz caster sugar
2 eggs, beaten
125 g/5 oz self-raising flour, sifted
Butter cream
100 g/4 oz butter, softened
225 g/8 oz sifted icing sugar
2 tablespoons cold milk

Set the oven at moderately hot (190 C, 375 F, gas 5).

Cream the butter or margarine with the sugar until light and fluffy. Beat in the eggs with a little of the flour. Carefully fold in the remaining flour.

Spoon into 18 paper bun cases set in bun tins. Bake in the heated oven for 20-25 minutes or until well risen and golden. Cool on a wire rack. When cool, cut a slice off the top of each cake and cut the slices in half. Top each cake with a swirl of butter cream made by creaming the butter with the icing sugar and milk. Placed the halved slices in the butter cream to form 'wings'. Dust lightly with a little sifted icing sugar.

Index